MW01485575

We would like to encourage the idea of
an interactive
cooperative relationship
between realms or levels of awareness.

We invite you to consider our perspective.
You are not asked to believe, but to consider.

Your innate wisdom will guide you to accept
only that to which you are aligned.

Allow yourself the gift of exploration

Orion

THE
ORION
MATERIAL

Perspectives of Awareness

20th Anniversary Edition

The Orion Material –
Perspectives of Awareness

20ᵗʰ Anniversary Edition

ISBN 978-0-944370-03-2

Library of Congress Control Number

2007903778

Spirituality

This book was developed and produced by

Synchronicity Press

Box 1154

Waynesboro, VA 22980 USA

www.synchronicitypress.com

Synchronicity - the sense of significance beyond chance

Cover Art on all editions from the painting
Clouded Conscience by Heidi Prescott
with gracious permission of the artist

Cover Design & Author Photo 2007
by Leslie France
www.bluewebweaver.com

Cover Art Photograph 2007 by Deb Booth
www.differentlightstudio.com

Printed in the United States of America

The
ORION
MATERIAL

Perspectives of Awareness

20th Anniversary Edition

2007

Elisabeth Y. Fitzhugh

Sʏɴᴄʜʀᴏɴɪᴄɪᴛʏ ᴘʀᴇss

Waynesboro, Virginia

CONTENTS

Realize there are layers of reality,
patterns of existence and consciousness,
realms of connectedness and understanding
which are not statically existing, but in motion.

This motion is flowing with vitality
and you are part of this Multiverse.
We ask you to live your life with complexity.
We ask that you know that each thing
is never just as it seems.

FOREWORD

Consider that we are more than our physical bodies, and thus can perceive and know more than the readily available physical world. Consider that we exist in a flow of intelligent consciousness that we can connect with and express. Consider a process whereby a person allows the opening of inner pathways or channels to receive such an expression. This is the Orion experience.

We understand Orion to be an expression of the intelligent consciousness we are all aspects of. Orion has a very special ability to articulate in neutral language the issues humanity finds hardest to deal with, be they personal or global. Their message of the All – the interconnectedness of all things – shines a spotlight on how we maintain the illusion of distance from ourselves and our world. Orion offers a resonance to support our capacity to transcend to further awareness as we also embrace and include our life's journey, just as it is, so far. Orion always shares as an interaction and exchange of equal value between realms of awareness, consistently presenting a non-dogmatic, inspiring view of reality, with dynamically useful and applicable information oriented toward evoking your own recognition and resonance with expanded awareness.

It was quite a surprise to discover that is has been twenty years since the publication of *The Orion Material – Perspectives of Awareness*. While deeply immersed in the most recent book based on the Orion material, *Dancers Between Realm – Empath Energy, Beyond Empathy*, we came to the final copies in stock of *The Orion Material*, and as we considered reprinting, we noted that the 20th anniversary was in 2007. Time markers often take us unaware and it was a special moment to realize this work has been shared for more than two decades.

As I began the task of reformatting and editing this edition, I was taken by the freshness and vitality of the material. The principles inherent in the Orion work – Unity, Interconnection, levels of Awareness and more – are presented succinctly in Orion's interactive way. The body of work we call the 'Orion Material' emerged in dialogue with participants in personal sessions, classes lectures and workshops. Although I knew that *Dancers Between Realms* was built upon the continuum of the Orion Material, refining and extrapolating earlier conversations and entering into new ones, the contiguous flow of energy between the two books struck me anew.

Orion enters into relationship with those who are drawn to them. In the one-to-one sessions, Orion easily renews connection and responds from the whole of a person, even if years intervene between actual sessions. Individual work with them consistently grows and deepens and many people share with me their own sense of how current sessions feel different than earlier ones. Orion continues to focus on integration and this, too, is shared with me by those who work with them individually, in classes, etc. Orion is also always learning with us and following their own axiom that we all speak to and for each other, embrace certain turns of phrase or metaphors or techniques that clients share with them in the context of sessions and classes.

Naturally, there have been changes in the Orion work. The language has fluidity; the material has found other levels of sophistication and depth. Rooted in the personal nature of Orion's interaction with individuals, the work is often expressed as a spiritual psychology. The orientation in this is that by exploring our own inner depths and truths, we can come to a further understanding of the nature of humanity and in seeing more and more clearly, can open to comprehending more than we at first know. I feel this growth is also reflected in the spiritual maturity of those who choose to explore with Orion. In the 80's many facets of spiritual awareness were opening to a new and broader audience than ever before. So much so, that a new genre of books and workshops was coined, 'New Age.' Today, individuals often bring a familiarity with spiritual precepts and vocabulary to their explorations, as well as discernment and a willingness to be self-aware and responsible. More aware participants are open to a wide-ranging exchange.

It has been a gift to be a participant in this exploration with the Orion consciousness. My own experience of them has broadened and although I still experience them as a thoughtful, caring energy with a personal expression uniquely their own, I now tend to think of them in a more transpersonal way, as an intelligent consciousness. My journey with them has truly been one of exploring new perspectives. Just as important has been developing the capacity to *not* know, to be willing to explore without a defined goal or purpose, to actually allow myself to discover, to look again, to change an idea or reframe a sense.

Not knowing and not needing to know, but being willing to see and consider that you may come to understand later, is one of the greatest gifts you can discover. In the end, mystery and the unknowable, in language and thought, are woven into the thread of being. The 21st century is open before us offering new paths of discovery as well as the opportunity to deepen our recognition of enduring principles of the inherent interconnection of all things. Perhaps we shall find ways, as individuals and society, to live from that very principle. Perhaps Unity shall find a way to be expressed consistently in the cultures of the world. This may not come to be in a global way, but we can surely express this heartbeat of being within our individual lives, one person at a time. *The Orion Material – Perspectives of Awareness* can serve as a gentle reminder of this possibility.

Elisabeth Y. Fitzhugh
2007

This edition has been reformatted and, in some instances, edited from earlier editions. Included is the Foreword and Glossary from the 2nd edition.

FOREWORD FROM ORION

FROM THE SECOND EDITION

1992

There was a time of conceiving.
Now there is a time of constructing.

As we look back on this book, compiled and drawn together by Elisabeth, we are aware that it is quite a foundation. The book is a rather concise presentation of many years of work. It is a capturing of principles for you to explore, to grow to understand, to have resonate with you.

The work represented in this book began in the early Eighties, which was very much a time of exploration and expansion. It was a time of people exploring new ideas and experiences; a time of people allowing themselves to take a step beyond everyday reality. Some have criticized this time period as being ego-centered. We think of it more as a time of discovery of the many variations within the self.

The Eighties was a time to allow experience, and those exploring the metaphysical world allowed themselves many and varied experiences. Some chose to work with ancient cultures. Others chose to work with elements of nature, such as herbs or stones or crystals. Others allowed new psychological discoveries. It was a time of new ways of relating emotionally; new ways of healing and balancing; a time to uncover inner discoveries and understanding.

We saw a time of many teachers coming in many forms – through this process called channeling and through a more subtle channeling process, inspiration. A time of inspired writing, intuitive art and intuitive expression in many ways. For many, the decade was a heady time filled with experience, catharsis and a panorama of doorway after doorway opening and individuals stepping through such doorways to new realms, new ideas.

Exploration simply to explore does have its limits.

Yet after a time, quite naturally, there comes a need to have a time of focus. Constant searching is like only eating desserts. How wonderful! How scrumptious! How exotic, perhaps. A special occasion! But in time you would crave something more substantial. The body would call for elements that create energy in a more fueling way. You would ask for protein. You would ask for fruits and vegetables. You would require substance; food that not only exhilarates, excites and stimulates the body, but supports it, sustains it, maintains it and allows it to grow and continue.

A time to create a supportive foundation
for working with new understanding,
for building upon knowledge.

The era before us is a time of focus. We see this as a time of structure; structure as a supportive foundation for working with new understanding; building upon applied knowledge. We are well aware that many people experience 'focus' and 'structure' as words that seem confining or limiting. We ask you to look at these words again; shift your perspective and consider structure anew.

Focus does not mean you close your eyes and senses to all around you. It does not mean limits. Rather, it means you choose to discern where you will place your energies. It reminds you that sometimes to sustain a certain path over time, to engage in a certain exploration, that path or exploration must have your attention. It must have your focus. The time of this focus may vary. It may be a focus for a few months or years. For others of you, your focus may engage you for the rest of your lives.

So many of you see structure as a limitation thrust upon you by outside forces; as something the outside world or society places upon you, drawing you away from your own direction and desires. Structure can be experienced like that, but think instead of structure as an armature. Envision structure as a sturdy foundation. When your foundation is well-built, in alignment and created with focus, it can support a great towering expanse of growth, of exploration and *application* – which brings ideas and ideals into actualized, concrete reality.

Consider a time of consistent application –
living what you have explored and have come to understand.

Take your spiritual explorations – your spiritual awareness and experiences, the connection you have felt with All There Is – and bring it to and weave it within your everyday world. Consider a time of *integration*, when what you have studied and experienced in extraordinary moments becomes not only special moments within your life, but threads weaving throughout all of your life.

In integration, extraordinary moments of knowing
will be the master thread – weaving, linking and flowing
throughout the patterns of your life.

As you develop integration, that extraordinary connection you experienced on Mt. Shasta; when you were in the pyramids in Egypt; when you felt the merging with the crystal world at Mt. Ida – these extraordinary times of comprehension and understanding will no longer stand alone as simply shining moments of life experience. They will flow throughout the all of your life. When you find yourself at your job, with your friends or with your parents or children – in all of the situations that seem separate from what you think of as your spiritual or mystical path – know that they are not in any way separate.

Know, again, that life is a great tapestry and that this is a time in which you are aware of being the weaver; of holding the needle and the thread. Think of the single thread of your spiritual awareness as a golden thread moving through every aspect of your life. See the thread outlining, supporting life and enhancing life, as the pattern you are weaving is guided by Unity.

What you are asked to bring to these times is your consciousness, accountability, and responsibility to allow the awareness you have explored and the expansion you have experienced to touch *all* of the aspects of your life. We remind you to see life holistically. Do not create a polarity or walk in separation and perhaps, judgment, of those who explore the spiritual and those who do not. Resist the path of 'us and them' that can become prevalent. Remember, *all* are of the spiritual. It is simply that you have chosen to consciously explore this aspect of being. Embrace holism. Hold dear the idea of life being interwoven with all aspects. Hold strong the goal of the integration of the spiritual view with the mundane and know that you best teach that which you share by living your life as an example.

The mystical experience is not to be held as an isolated, precious moment.

Allow consistent practical application of what you have learned. Your mystical experiences, the sensing of All There Is, are not to be held as separate treasures. Indeed, you may experience precious moments, but such times are tools, practical devices, mechanisms and catalysts for creating understanding and comprehension – tools to bring knowledge and awareness to be shared, not aggrandized. Share this awareness not only in language but in your actions.

Think of yourselves not as simply
part of the Universe, but as part of a Multiverse.

Realize there are layers, moving patterns, realms of connectedness and understanding – not statically existing, but in motion. This motion is flowing with vitality and you are part of this Multiverse. We ask you to live your life with complexity. We ask that you know that each thing is never just as it seems.

This is what I understand now, but I acknowledge
there can be more than I perceive.

Now, it may be that to live life one must accept focus. One must work with an idea as if it is not in motion and mutable. But we ask you to hold to the idea that 'This is what I understand now, but I acknowledge there can be more than I perceive.' Affirming that there may be that which you do not know is a very empowering and supportive idea. It is a concept that prevents rigidity. It is a reminder that you may come to another view. This affirmation supports and allows change, movement, shifts. It is a reminder that mutability is inherent in the nature of reality.

In this book we refer to spiritual pioneers as those who live their lives in integration with their spiritual principles. You may be among them. These pioneers are not only traveling to discover new conceptual places and new lands of thought, they are beginning to homestead, creating and building through the application of their knowledge and experience. You may not be building farms and towns and cities, yet you do build. You may demonstrate new ways to approach problem-solving. Others share new views of working to balance the body. Still others teach new ways of relating. This is a frontier of consciousness – of ideas and thoughts. We see a frontier of exploring, demonstrating that how we change our thinking does create viable alternatives in action. We feel it is a time of invigorating vitality of application.

**Use your experience of the inner world
to support you in the outer world.**

New applications and skills, vital expressions of the integration of spiritual awareness, are especially needed in these times. The expansiveness of the past few decades may seem unavailable now. But do not be overwhelmed by the illusion of lack, of loss. Rather, recognize there are times of change; a time that may ask you to change. Like children who come into their own sense of mastery through challenge and responsibility – through earning their own money or being responsible for another – the spiritual pioneers come into a fuller sense of connectedness and mystic mastery through application.

**Allow your spiritual understandings
to support you through challenge.**

You may find there are times when you must discover new ways of working in the world. These are times when you seem bound by what is. These are times when affirming the flow of energy – such as making an affirmation to receive money – does not generate that flow as easily as before. Do not be so quick to hold yourself to blame, but consider that this is a different time, a different clime. Consider that this very difference, which is present, may simply be requiring you to act differently.

Do not be afraid to dance with *all* the energies in life.
You have the strength and wisdom
of All There Is to dance with you.

Knowing the ways of the Multiverse does not guarantee a life of ease and abundance, as is sometimes thought. Rather, this knowledge offers continual support through whatever challenge may arise; a deep support that is available through the experience of connection to All There Is and the understandings that naturally flow from that connection. Living in connection with spirit is the foundation to support you in experiencing all the paths of life, even those perceived as slow, arduous, or difficult. Do not base your spiritual exploration on a search for a life of ease or on fear of life's challenges. Do not be afraid to dance with all the energies in life, difficult as well as joyous. You have the strength and wisdom of All There Is to dance with you.

Allow your personal explorations
to grow roots in the mundane.

Embrace a time of constructing practical, applied actions and attitudes rooted in your far-ranging explorations, realizations and discoveries. The explorer who does not build a settlement, who does not apply the knowledge gleaned from travel, is eventually doomed only to travel and observe. But it is through the application of new ideas and different views, when others experience the continual demonstration of your knowledge, that the sharing begins and the building commences. To us, personal discovery inherently holds the seed of teaching and sharing and the responsibility to nurture that seed.

Sharing creates an experience of Unity. Those who consistently experience that they are connected to all things eventually cannot live in separation from each other and their world. We invite you to walk with us and others like us to explore and apply many ways of learning, knowing and discovering. Your strength lies in your continued recognition of Unity.

Orion 1991

We are all together.
We are all linked.
We are all inherently
part of All There Is.
Therein lies our strength,
wisdom, and compassion.
Unity is.

ON CHANNELING

Channeling is a phenomenon that is often misunderstood and is, for some, unsettling. Yet, channeling is increasing these days, with more and more information and awareness available via the channeling process. Simply put, channeling is a process whereby a person 'opens' inner pathways or 'channels' to receive information from outside the conscious mind, perhaps from beyond our known reality. This open state is most often achieved through some sort of meditative or expansion process, an altered state on the part of the receiver, which facilitates receptivity.

The cornerstone of understanding channeling is to consider the concept that we are more than our physical bodies, and thus, we can perceive more than the physical world. A concept such as this opens the way for acceptance of the possibility of contacting and receiving information from other existences or realms of being. Reading channeled material is an experiential choice – one either 'resonates' with or feels connected to a book or not. One senses that the material is or is not relevant for one's own development. The increasing variety of material available offers a wide choice of perspectives.

Orion sees people as fully capable of individually choosing information that is useful and valid. Orion emphasizes our ability to synthesize our own belief structure from all that we study and experience, using our innate wisdom as a tool of discernment. In this book, Orion offers their broad perspective for your consideration, expressly encouraging you to accept and integrate within yourself only that to with which you are aligned.

The Orion Material is an edited compilation of sessions with Orion recorded over several years. The material was gathered in various types of sessions: from individual personal sessions, to a class format, through large-scale public lectures. Some of the material was initiated and presented as a whole by Orion. Other material evolved through Orion's response to individual questions and requests. This *interactive* element, where topics presented grow from the input of the participants, is an important aspect of the Orion work.

The merged energy of Orion shares a highly expanded perspective through the channel of Elisabeth Y. Fitzhugh. We have understood Orion to be a group of five non-physical beings who follow their own spiritual path by providing guidance and information. This is, indeed, our understanding of these beings, but we cannot say it is the definite statement of fact on the nature of Orion. When we accept the possibility of communication and connection between differing realities, we must also acknowledge that we deal with our own interpretations of the information and realities we connect with. Any sharing of realities, be they human cultures or other dimensions, holds the possibility of misunderstanding.

We present to you our understanding of who and what Orion are, and while you may be comfortable with our view, it is not necessary for you to believe in Orion as we understand them. Rather, we invite you, as Orion invites you, to consider the content of the material presented, discerning for yourself the value of the information, in and of itself. We find the Orion perspective to be a valuable and viable view for our times. Orion began their sharing by touching the personal lives of a few. They share a non-dogmatic, expanded perspective which now has facilitated growth and expansion for many.

The personal quest for exploration is still with us. Let us consider the possibility of other realms of existence, other dimensions, and other planetary realities. Let us embrace the idea that communication and exchange between unseen worlds is a viable possibility for exploration. In ancient times, receiving information from beyond the self was a matter of course. Life has taken us far from listening to such guidance and, now, back again. The hallmark of our times lies in developing the ability to integrate our expanded technologies and knowledge with a consideration of the inner essence, including wisdom from sources that do not fit our current scientific explanations and understanding.

Orion reminds us to honor ourselves in our willingness to explore new perspectives. Orion honors us as spiritual pioneers. We accept the pioneers within us and offer this book to the pioneers within you.

Synchronicity Press 1987

CHAPTER ONE

ORION ON ORION

*We do not declare that our view is the totality
or The Truth or in any way the
definitive statement on what we see.
It is simply our perspective.*

We are presenting some of our views of expanded awareness, and you will indeed find that our view holds similar elements of many other philosophies, world views and universal views you have already incorporated into your own awareness. Our presentation may not be radically unique in all aspects, but perhaps you will find it resonates with you in a way that may bring more integration of such ideas and principles into your awareness and consciousness than you have heretofore experienced. This is not to say we are trying in any way to supersede other teachings, other techniques, or other speakers that are in your lives. We do not seek to be a Master Teacher, The Master Teacher, or offer a Master Way. It is not within our view that there is a singular option or way.

As Orion, we are a group of five separate energies who have chosen to blend together and present this work. Although we work in what we call, a 'merged state', we are not blended into one nondifferentiated being. We have chosen to work through Elisabeth with her conscious agreement. At her request, we have chosen one energy of our whole as spokesperson. This speaker represents the thought of our group.

We are asked, 'Would you, Orion, be capable of speaking through a person other than Elisabeth?' Capable, perhaps yes. Presently, though, we choose to work only through her, continuing our relationship with her. Usually the specific energy or energies that align with an individual in the channeling modality come present through agreement between the channel and those channeled. This agreement is made in the expanded self, as well as in the present conscious self. We see channeling as facilitated through a specific alignment that actually is in the physical.

Our view is that Elisabeth's form, as an example, at forming, at birth, had certain elemental, cellular adjustments attuning her being for this work. Always, though, one is allowed the opportunity to accept or reject, to choose to interact or not with the channeling relationship, but the bodily form is prepared. Most often a commitment to the channeling relationship is on a one-to-one basis. The duration may be a time in one's life, a lifetime or many lifetimes. Channeled information often resonates with that which is being presented by others such as us at the same time. These varied presenters offer a choice of energy alignment. Some of what we share will be new and unique to you. Other elements we share will resonate with other speakers and teachers with whom you have come in contact. In our view, this element of choice is the nature of the channeling process. As in much of your society, there are great degrees of choice.

> Personal channeling of awareness is
> a different phenomenon than the full
> channeling of the energy of the
> beings themselves.

It is possible that information can be received from other realities by many individuals in a manner which does not involve the full channeling of beings or energy through the physical form. Thus, it is possible for individuals to experience their own connection with such as us when individuals allow a certain relationship or linking. Such linking is facilitated through connecting with the material being shared, as in participating in seminars or classes, or reading or hearing the channeled sharings. In this way, people often experience a connection or message from beings that are being channeled through others. Basically, it is possible that information can be received from such as us in a manner that does not involve the full channeling of the energy through the physical form.

> Our group, Orion, represents
> an echo of a view of awareness from many.

As you find in your reality, many teachers from other realities are presenting information that is similar or is congruent. The idea and need for many teachers is simple. There are many vibrations, many levels of awareness, much differentiation available. There are those we are aligned with and those we will reach, that another teacher will not reach in the same way. It is, quite simply, another choice. We remind you that all the principles we talk of are really constructs of thinking, structures of comprehension. We share knowledge to a certain degree and we see each of you as fully capable of adding to that knowledge.

Our work is based on exchange.

We do not hold to the idea that beings in form are here only to learn and that all knowledge and awareness is extant, waiting to be learned. You are missing the mark! Each of you has a great validity, not only in your own life but in the greater scheme of all things. It is within the realms of possibility, moving towards *probability*, that one of you or many of you, will be able to receive or create an understanding, a presentation, an addition to concepts we are sharing or that others share. Already we have had individuals present to us ways of phrasing examples of understanding that are highly attuned and accurate and we have incorporated these explanations into our work. Our work is based on exchange and we hope this does not diminish the experience for you.

We are interested in the activation and energization of your abilities to link with the core essence of awareness within you.

We will say that through the nature of our being, our perspective is broader perhaps, than that which is readily available to you. Yet, we remind you again, that it is quite possible you will be that being who will add another element, make another link, in the ever continuing exploration of the nature of all beings and the nature of reality. We are not an authority. All that we say is to be judged, in the most positive way of discernment, by each individual. Rather than you quoting our words, what we are more interested in is the activation and energization of your abilities to link in with the core essence of awareness within you.

**We are evolutions and embodiments
of many explorations through life expressions.**

The main speaker of Orion was at one time of the human form in a civilization not yet known in your historical time. It was a culture akin to Native American, in the area of South America, but which was in a different physical position than at present. This was a nature-oriented society and culture. Also, this being experienced other timings and other planets not in your known history. The life expressions in form of the speaker were also linked with life expressions in other planetary systems, followed by periods of time not in form. Other elements of the group Orion have had some similarity of expressions, but not in the earth form, although there have been connections with the Earth planet. It is our understanding that there are reality systems existing in the vibrational fields of planets, in addition to the form systems of the planets themselves.

Those of us who have joined the group Orion exist as individual vibrations in a system of vibration that has association with this planet and others. Our energies separately are individuated and have linkages with other serving or teaching groups besides Orion. As Orion we work with our five elements only. One comes to existences such as ours usually after experiencing various forms of living. We are evolutions and embodiments of many explorations through life expressions.

**There is an energy on the planet of
more individuals coming into receptivity.**

We are asked, 'What are some of the background reasons for the many channels and types of channeling now appearing?' We feel there is an energy on the planet of more individuals coming into receptivity and ability to have more consideration of exchange of energy. Much of this has been brought about by degrees of physical security and health that have been produced in certain societies on the planet. An element of freedom from physicality is one aspect that very often permits this kind of expansion. We do not necessarily mean that there have to be high levels of existence, but even in the nature cultures that have experienced great interconnection with other levels, those small cultures were usually very supported by the environment. Thus, a certain abundance led to physical security, which helps facilitate the exploration beyond the physical reality. These elements are present in your time and place.

You are not asked to believe, but to consider.

We invite you to consider our perspective. We ask you to honor the sense that may have drawn you to this sharing of our view. Those who choose to share or choose to teach, are most fulfilled when there are those who likewise choose to listen, to participate with them. Like the artist, we will share and offer even if we are not heard. But, the idea and the thrust of our path is communication, and communication is a medium of exchange. Join us in our exploration by offering your energy of consideration and receptivity.

Your innate wisdom will guide you
to accept only that
which is aligned to you.

Allow yourself
the gift of
exploration.

CHAPTER TWO

UNITY

You are already part of any perfection
you visualize outside of you.
You are your unique expression of it.
You are this note in the symphony and
you are essential for the symphony.

The Unity is literally All There Is. It entails in part linking in with each other, to link into the energies that represent thoughts and ideas, knowledge and facts, experiences and opportunities. You are all part of a Wholeness. You are wholeness. It is your right, by the nature of your being, to experience conscious connection with what we call the perfection within. In and of itself, the single cell – the hologram of the entire body – is a small perfection, a small world; it experiences itself as a wholeness.

You have agreed to become a separate being. You have agreed to interact with the reality of form: a reality that can set you reeling, that can be difficult or stressful. You have agreed to interact with realities where patterns evolve that you cannot discern or fully understand. Within this agreement, we remind you, one has not given up one's connectedness with perfection and harmony. You have not given up your connection with knowledge and with power. You have the right to experience these elements of connection, to tap into them, to be sustained by them. You have the right to experience the wholeness of all being.

By the nature of your reality, however, you will not experience this kind of unity at all times. You have chosen to be in an active, moving, volatile element of life. But you do have the ability to access, to touch, to link through yourself to All There Is as you need to, when you need to.

We remind you also, in times of need, you can find support to touch into Unity by reaching within and also by calling upon energies outside of yourselves. Call upon sharers such as us. Call upon those elements you experience as your guides. Reach out to whatever energy source you wish to call upon. Each of you is fully capable of receptivity and linking with such energy sources and you may experience this connection is many ways – visual communications, verbal sensations, experiential or subtle awareness. We remind you of your ability to initiate this connection and your choice to do so in a manner you decide best, such as meditation, prayer, or dialogue. Remember, though, these connections may be subtle and indirect, in the realm of feeling and sensing rather than what you would consider a more direct experience.

THE WEB

**The idea of working with energy is to know there are
webs of understanding, webs of energy
in your world, other worlds, the universe—
that you cannot fathom.**

The Web is not yours to fathom. One may never get the full view. Even those such as us who have an expanded view do not have the full and complete view. Know that total understanding may not be known, for expansion and evolution in All There Is continues. Webs of interconnection weave through each life, each reality. Thus, any practice you engage in where your conscious mind attempts to direct your desires and their outcomes to very specific ends by your control of energies, can have effects and ramifications you had not anticipated; results you do not desire; consequences you had not imagined. The reason is that you simply do not have all of the available information about a situation. It is our perspective that when people get into uncomfortable situations, through energy manipulation, through rigidly specific visualization, it is because they are attached to an outcome determined by their conscious desires alone. They have not taken into consideration the interweaving of The Web.

**Be willing to set a direction –
but not to force the direction of the energy.**

In all spiritual exploration, we recommend a willingness to let go of the will, a willingness to move with the unseen webs you may not consciously understand. Be willing to set a direction, perhaps hold an expectation, but not force the direction of the energy. Let yourself direct energy without trying to determine the final outcome. It is appropriate to manage and move energy, but to then attempt to direct it in a specific manner can have its mishaps. Be willing to work in the idea of what you might call Higher Power or Source, the idea that there is some kind of meaning and form and pattern in your universe that you do move within, tap into, and access. Honor the webs of interconnection. We cannot stress this element of exploration too much. It is the subtle key of directing your intent, yet letting go of coercing the outcome. One does not seek. One permits and then allows awareness to come present.

THE TRIAD OF AWARENESS
Inner Awareness
Expanded Awareness
Conscious Awareness

The main principle we are bringing in our teaching is integration. In our terminology, we refer to three levels of awareness. You will find at least a semblance of this in other philosophies as well.

We speak of the Inner Awareness. Inner Awareness takes you to realms of intuitiveness. Inner Awareness is the realm of intuition, sensing, as well as control of the body in certain emotional planes. In our view, an aspect of Inner Awareness is what we call the Creator spark, the soul, the inner essence, which is the aspect containing all-knowingness. The Core Essence is that element within each of you that is aware and knowing of its connection with all life, all energy and all creation. This Core Essence is keenly aware of your personal direction: where you have come from, where you may choose to go. Coupled with the Inner Awareness, is the Conscious Awareness, or ego awareness. Ego is the conscious expression of the personality in your present life.

Beyond that, we have the Expanded Awareness. The Expanded Awareness, sometimes known as Higher Self, is that aspect of you which can reach out beyond your physical being and can link with what is called the mass consciousness. It is the aspect capable of linking with the cosmic consciousness. You have the ability through the Expanded Awareness to touch all aspects of being. As you can see, in our view, the Expanded Awareness directly relates to the Inner Awareness and the inner knowing core. You can consider the Expanded Awareness that element which flows from your intent to reach out in action, to gather in knowledge and understanding. Again, you are part of All There Is. The Core Essence connects all elements. Through the Core Essence you have the innate ability to connect with, link with, and gather information from and awareness of many, many levels of understanding of this reality and other realities as well.

Intuition and hunch, synchronicity and coincidence –
all of these terms are reflections of a natural law,
the natural way people work.

Awareness is literally a flow of energy. You will find life easier when you connect the inner awareness receptivity and the expanded awareness outreach with conscious awareness. As you cooperate with this natural flow and the ability to touch into and be connected with All There Is a wide range of understanding and comprehension becomes more readily available. You discover clarity of what you must focus on or decide. People call it 'the flow', and it *is* a flow of energy.

> **The Inner Awareness is more than the personality
> you are at present, more than the personality
> you are expressing now.**

Psychology, on the other hand, suggests a model that within a calm, rational person there is always a seething pit of confusion, the unconscious. So, as people try to learn to trust their feelings, sensings, and their inner-knowings, they hold a fear of tricking themselves. There is a fear of being wrong, of playing some game on the self, and of being tripped up in the end by the negatives within the unconscious.

We describe this psychologically-defined element of the unconscious as the psychological matrix. There may be ambivalence, confusion and resistance present in the psychological matrix. Remember, though, that the psychological explanation is itself an idea, a conceptualization of the nature of emotions, a construct of one way of understanding. In the psychological modality, the unconscious is embedded in the personality. We see it as an aspect of your totality.

The key to allowing inter-connectedness is to accept the idea of the perfection of your Core Essence.

A key for each of you to more fully come into touch with the interconnectedness of all beings and things is the *surrender* – the giving up of negative images of the self, the giving up of the idea that you are a poor creature. The key is to accept the idea of the perfection of your Core Essence. The challenge is to move more and more consistently into everyday expression of contact with your Core Essence of perfection. You are wise beings who have the ability to lead yourselves accurately with love, caring, and sensitivity. The trust you seek from outside yourself must come first and foremost from within. As you begin to demonstrate to yourself what you have created through working with all your levels of awareness, you will build a system of trust. This trust is a great gift to you.

BUILDING A HISTORY OF AWARNESS

Inner Awareness holds an accuracy of knowledge you can learn to identify and trust.

When we talk about inner knowing we are talking again of that deep element, that spark, that connecting force which may be as small as an atom or element in your science, which unites all of us with the all of it, All There Is. This includes thoughts, ideas, concepts, probabilities, actualities, etc. All is energy. We are not saying you should not use discernment or conscious understanding. The goal is *integration*. We are saying you should not dismiss out of hand your own intuitive senses. Hold the idea of the cooperative nature of your whole being participating in processing information: Conscious Awareness, Inner Awareness, and Expanded Awareness working together in a moving, sharing, interactive relationship.

You are not asked to simply believe ideas on interconnection. We want you to learn to demonstrate it to yourself, and build your own empirical history of accuracy.

Every time you've had a hunch and you followed it through and it worked – note it. Every time you went back to buy the briefcase you saw in the window which felt just right, but talked yourself out of and finally acknowledged your sense was correct, but the briefcase was gone – note it! Every time you have the sense a direction or choice is coming to you make note of it. What you are doing here is building your own conscious history of how you are fully and naturally able to work with a broader receiving system than your conscious mind.

The conscious mind is a tool of discernment.

The conscious mind is the tool of discernment which brings inner sensings into a consciously understood concept which can then be created into a form or action. By the nature of its need to hold focus, the conscious mind has a narrower view than the Inner Awareness. Thus, inner knowings have a broader view. Sometimes the energy is so mutable you only have a *sense* of a situation. This is because the energy literally is not yet dense enough to be formed into a thought or a concept. Again, we invite you to begin trusting the information you receive. Build the empirical history of 'I had a sense and I followed it through and it proved correct.' Let yourself observe the consistent accuracy of all of these things, these coincidences and synchronicities. You will build for yourself a base of knowledge demonstrating that you can work with these inner senses accurately.

Do not fear you will give up your abilities of judgment and discernment.

Rather than thinking of this way of understanding as an 'either/or' situation, as conscious thought versus inner knowing, begin to allow yourself to think of it as a moving, coalescing process. See it as an interactive process of the Inner Awareness, the Conscious Awareness and the Expanded Awareness. As you have thoughts and feelings about an issue, remember you do not have to take immediate action on your Inner Awareness. You need only *consider* what comes to you. Begin to let yourself experience yourself as a wise person. Allow yourself to consider that if you are not a wise person, perhaps you have a speck of wisdom in you. Begin there.

The Core Essence, which you access through Inner Awareness,
is a conduit of information and awareness;
of feeling the pathways of the Web.

Do you know what responsibility is? We call it respond-ability. It is not a great weight of having to do things you do not want to do. It means you are willing to have the ability to respond to a situation in a certain way. When you talk of drawing things into your life – be it information, a person, or a new job – you are talking of the natural process of using innate elements as tools to link with All There Is. It is our view that this link is of a wholly positive nature, and that the impetus for almost all actions of a person is to serve the being. Now it is true that sometimes the original impetus becomes altered and the effect no longer serves. The protective reaction of withdrawal you created as a child of five, may no longer serve you in the same way at age thirty. But we talk of this positive impetus so you will be able to hold the concept that the core of your being is positive, has the capacity to draw in wisdom, accurate information and knowingness that is aligned with you.

Thus, if you can consider all of these premises, you are then ready to consider the idea that when information of a choice comes present to you very, very strongly, it may well be an energy that is truly accurate, aligned and linked with you. It may be a choice that you have already, perhaps, made in the reaches of The Web. You can simply touch in and ask yourself. Listen to the answers your self gives. The greatest difficulty most people have is in accepting the validity of the answers, the knowledge they receive.

17

Many people are receptive to the information. They then choose to judge it or dismiss it or fear it or not trust it.

Let us make clear in another way why we feel the information gleaned through your Inner Awareness is trustworthy. Consider again the concept of the Core Essence, the crystal of, can we say, Source, Creator, the Divine, whatever term you choose. More simply, and in less mystical terms, consider this element as a pulsation that links and enables you to link, with all others, with living creatures, with all matter, with All There Is. It is an element we all share an essence of, no difference if a being or energy is in form or not in form. We are all connected from the same place. The Core Essence which you access through Inner Awareness is a conduit of information and awareness, of feeling the pathways of the Web.

**The Innate Wisdom is a delightfully
wonderful and accurate sensory tool,
particularly for you about you.**

When information starts coming at you from all sides, as they say, it is again because the information is literally surrounding you as energy. It is the information connected to you within The Web. Thus, when other energies – other people, other things – come into your system, they will reflect back to you the energy of information pertinent to your vibration. It is a wonderful system. It reinforces itself. Listen. Consider the information. But do remember, what people say to you may not be the literal information to take action on. For instance, someone may say, 'Oh, your hair is so dramatic!' or 'I don't like your hair!' or 'Your hair really does things to me!' Such information could mean you might consider changing your hairstyle or your response could be your recognition that this expression of you is something you really like and you are going to hold to it no matter how others feel about it. Look at feedback in all different ways. Examine what the data means to you. Do not immediately react to the response. Consider. Accept the information, but don't necessarily accept the judgment or the connotation that might be given with it.

Remember, sensings from innate wisdom are especially attuned to you. You should use clear and balanced discernment before you offer any firm opinion to others on your sensings for them. But for yourself, since that matrix of knowledge is so attuned to you, is a part of you and is linked to all you are, the inner sensings are highly refined tools of awareness and will demonstrate consistent accuracy. The more you can align your conscious mind with accepting the validity of this inner wisdom, the more you will find yourself aligned easily and naturally to the rhythms of your life.

The difficulty for people working with Inner Awareness is to doubt, judge, or dismiss the information received.

Your conscious mind or ego is a tool of discernment. It should always be used as a tool of discernment. Unfortunately, discernment out of balance leads to judgment. Judgment moves easily into resistance and resistance moves easily to blockage. If you find yourself judging, moving away from or doubting the information you have received, we ask that you take that healthy judgment, which we hope you think of as discernment, and visualize it within a locked box. Visualize the locked box placed on the shelf for a bit. You need not get rid of your judgment. You need not change it. You simply put it aside for a time and let the information flow uninhibited by limiting judgment.

Now you can reach your discernment and choice of action after you have received the information unfettered by your resistance to its accuracy and permitted some level of integration. Permit yourself to receive information. Allow time for the processing, thinking and recognizing awareness. The distillation of all these elements will emerge as integration and will come forward and be clear to you.

The Conscious Mind is a wonderful, useful and beautiful tool.

The Conscious Mind is not to be denigrated or dismissed. The Conscious Mind is that excellent tool which facilitates taking Inner Awareness and inner senses and bringing them into focus, form, and action. The unique element human beings bring is the creation of wonderful form and action of energy.

The spiritual path is allowing awareness to expand.

Aware people make use of all information to expand their view of their world. First, they have listened to the inner senses and they accept the validity of their own sensing and inner wisdom. This is the most difficult part of all, accepting that validity. Second, they are willing to record in their memory that their sensing was accurate. They are willing to recognize the whole flowing process. This is the spiritual path: allowing the awareness to expand. All that you study when you explore spiritual philosophy is of two parts. One, your Inner Awareness has brought something you are aligned to into your realm. Two, you have brought a way for your Conscious Mind to consider new concepts and ideas. The Conscious Mind, this divine tool, can also be very limited. Yet, the Conscious Mind is highly educable. You can expand the perimeters and the parameters of your thinking through permitting exploration of ideas.

Giving yourself freedom to explore can open new elements, new dimensions of the self. It does not mean that you must always take the action on the idea you think about or imagine. But, having permitted the exploration of the idea of choice in your mind and thoughts, gives you a strong structure, a strong foundation of information and knowledge, which supports your abilities to make choices, consider options and form your own understanding of the nature of reality.

This positive supporting energy of the Unity,
that you are a part of All There Is,
is always available, but it must
be accepted within and nurtured.

We ask you to see the travails of life, minor and major, as challenges and information bringers. We offer that the impetus for growth is always positive and, we would use the term, loving. We see this concept as another key to empowerment. Therefore, if you can allow this principle to flow through and to be integrated within your being, you will find it a great support factor in all situations you may become part of. This is not to say that such a concept will reduce all difficulties, or that you will not feel pain and disappointment, anger and frustration and such emotions. Rather, as you pass through the intensity of expressions, when you can take the moment to center, sit and listen, you may be able to use these ideas and tools to help you through whatever difficulty is being presented.

In times of desperation and alienation, remember there is always an element of positive energy within. There is positive energy available to you at all times. It is important to allow yourself to be your own best friend. A cliché, yes, but also a powerful axiom. Look to yourself to tap into strength through your Inner Awareness, so you may touch into a support of energy that all of your guilt and ambivalence cannot dilute.

This positive supporting energy of the Unity, mirrored in that you are part of All There Is, is always available to you, but it must be accepted within and nurtured. After a time you will find the positive energy without having to seek it. Society does not provide many tools for supporting oneself. The duality of your society is such that if you pat yourself on the back too much, there is something wrong and you are seen as conceited and vain and arrogant. Yet, it is also accepted that you love yourself.

We wish to assist you in recognizing,
more and more consistently,
the existence of your core of perfection.

Remember, this reality is a land of deep currents of seeming paradox, duality and ambivalence. Do not judge yourself when you move into ambivalence or negativity. Just allow the movement to be quicker. You will always be in motion. Challenges will come. Life is not static. What you are trying to develop is flexibility and fluidity, which can enable you to move easily through ambivalence, guilt and limitations. In this, you can use the energies of self-integrated reality, self-integrated spiritual truth, and the self-integrated truth of your own goodness and worth to support you in the deepest way.

This goodness and worth is *innate*, the reflection of the crystal of perfection we all share an element of. True, actions, words, and choices may not present perfection, but the core of perfection exists, even if it is not accessed or recognized. We wish to assist you in recognizing more and more consistently the existence of your core of perfection.

> **You all have wisdom.**
> **You are never only the student, the explorer.**
> **You are always the teacher and sharer as well.**

If we can give you anything, we would most like to give you the following two things. First, a strong idea, a strong concept that you can anchor into a root of support. You have wisdom within you. There is a guide within you. There is a link within you that can offer direction, lead you, call you, and move with you to certain paths, to certain choices, to certain awareness, to certain knowledge. Hold to the idea that you all have wisdom: Innate Wisdom. Your impulses are led by positive imperatives. There is always exchange.

Secondly, know that you are never only the student and explorer. You are always the teacher and sharer, as well. And paradoxically, you may serve as a teacher when you are sharing with no conscious intent of teaching at all. So often a friend may share how something you said really affected them and you find that you don't really remember what you said or even the context. This is a reminder to treasure our interactions with each other, to trust that when we are willing to share of ourselves, we may connecting with others in ways we do not know. Connection finds its way with and without our direction and purpose. The interconnectedness of Unity leads the flow of the web of interconnection.

AN AFFIRMATION TOWARDS UNITY

We extend energization towards
harmony, security, serenity.

An energization for each of you to
experience the flow of support, sustenance,
recognition and connection
which can be experienced through
your understanding and connecting
with the understanding of yourself.

Recognize you are part of more than yourself,
that you are linked with others,
that you are part of the whole.

Use the idea of
your interconnection
to support you.

CHAPTER THREE

SPIRITUAL AWARENESS

The spiritual path is not a seeking.
It is expressing the spiritual impulse that already exists
and bringing it into alignment and integration
with the conscious mind and everyday life.

The spiritual path is an aware choice. The one who is consciously exploring spiritual awareness is attempting more and more consistently and with regularity to make use of, to cooperate with, and to integrate the principles of this Inner Awareness into all that their life is. So the spiritual path is your life. It is integrated into all of your life. The spiritual path may simply be expressed as a fuller awareness of All There is. The spiritual path is expressing the innate spiritual impulse.

We really would like to encourage individuals to see that living itself is the expression of the spiritual impulse. Living is your spiritual path. We encourage you to bring your experiences and your development and your awareness, with integration of these elements as your thrust, to the living of your life. Please do not hold the misconception that being in touch with your spiritual essence or exploring expanded realities means that everything in your life will always be of perfection. Rather, it means that you will always be able to step out and give yourself a broad perspective so you can come to understand more of all the varieties of living. It isn't a guarantee of only happiness and prosperity. It is a tool to allow you a fuller participation in whatever comes to be created.

Many people hold to the idea of the spiritual path, and exploring spirituality as still linked to those images best evoked by a monastery. This idea embodies relinquishing, renouncing, giving up, focusing only on the spiritual practices as inherent in the expression of spirituality. We do not agree with this view. We feel that type of focus is of another time and place that does not serve very well most people in the present society and time.

We would like to see spirituality become an integral part of the fullness that a human life can create.

We hold to the energy of integral spirituality, rather than spirituality experienced and expressed through isolation and separation. Such integration would bring the spiritual principles to all things – to joy, to sex, to fun, to children, to political activism, to race car driving, to sports, to movies, to all the things that are aspects of the creation and creativity of the form and of this society you have been born into and are part of.

This is really the challenge. Why a challenge? Integrated spirituality cannot be worn like a badge, so it cannot really give the same kind of ego-identification as that which an overt and defined system of spirituality seems to declare. As an example, the monk is recognized. His robe says, 'Ah, we have a spiritual man here!' The young man with a fast car and a lady friend or two is not immediately and overtly recognized as a spiritual man. His spiritual expression is not being shown to the world in an immediately recognizable manner. It can be a challenge to have spirituality be that which you express within your life and not be readily recognized, respected and supported by others.

Each human being is connected with the creative force that is present in all beings.

We begin again with the premise that each human being is connected with the creative force that is present in all beings. In all life. In all existence. This could be called Source, Spirit, Creator energy, God. It need not be labeled or envisioned in such a specific manner. There is no singular perception. Rather, it is a current, a vibration within all perceptions. The main aspect of this which is of importance to the individual is, first, that this is your birthright. When you created this life in this form, this inner vibration was present with you. It is of you. This you need not seek or find. It is present.

This inner vibration also is a pulsator, a bearer of wisdom. A bearer of goodness. Each of you is inherently good. Inherently wise. This pulsation also has within it the ability of receiving, of receiving information and awareness from far beyond your conscious mind. From far beyond this physical reality. Each of you, no matter what you think, makes use of that receptive ability over and over again in life.

Every individual has had some experience where they have connected with The Web, the interconnection of all things. It may only be the time you answered the door two seconds before a friend arrives. 'Oh it was just ESP!' you declare. Everyone has allowed some such experience. We encourage you to grow in the awareness of these experiences. Begin through developing your awareness that there are these connections and experiences.

You will then grow into the level where you begin to allow yourself to work with the energy in attempting the integration, the balance of not simply receiving but also of sending, of initiating. It is always a subtle balance. It is balancing. You are never there. Even with death you are not there. The goal of 'getting there,' of completion, is not necessary. The importance is within the motion and the living.

The concept of a Wholistic view is taken from another level.

Life as 'wholistic' is a concept now integrating on this planet of duality. It is quite delightful that this challenge has been accepted. The idea of wholism is really a very radical term for this reality. Earth is a planet of duality. The physical reality is predominantly expressed as polarized aspects. In general, the wholistic concept is not being reflected back to you through nature, nor in the general manner of relating on your planet. Yet, the ideas of positive and negative, of polarity and the need to balance polarity, are not to be judged as you understand they also are reflections of the physicality that has evolved on this planet. Thus, it is truly a challenge to move beyond this physical nature. You should honor yourselves at your willingness to move into energy awareness and participation that is not reflective in the natural processes of your reality.

In our view, there is no great singular cosmic morality.

Morality structures are evolutions from societies and the forms of the beings and the planets where they are created and exist. As an example, there are too many kinds of differing realities for highly ordained strictures on sexual expression. As an example, a reality of beings having a single gender would not evolve moral structures around the issue of homosexuality, as this would be the nature of that reality. We accept the paradox that there are many seemingly opposite positions and views being presented as having validity. We ask that it be considered all as part of the whole.

We do not see destiny as being bound and determined. We see cycles of movement and we see that the webs of interaction are very complex indeed. Some of you may find this view unsettling; for others it may be empowering. Make use of it. If it is unsettling, sit with it, look at it again.

CO-CREATING REALITY

When you co-create your reality,
it honors the idea that there are
patterns and connections that interact
with your choices and awareness.
A system of interweaving,
a flexible, mutable pattern.
We call this The Web.

We hold the idea of co-creating reality. We accept the idea that there are certain 'webs' of movement. The Web is not an unchangeable destiny. The Web has certain indications, certain pulls. Indeed, an individual can be born to bring through a certain task, a certain service, a certain talent. But we see each individual as fully able to say yea or nay to working with that talent or service.

Co-creation honors the idea that there are patterns and connections that interact with your choices and awareness. See it as a system of interweaving flexible, mutable patterns of harmony. When you work to *co-create* your life, you bring a combination of your intent and will to a meeting place of certain parameters you may or may not fully recognize. The 'all of you' has certain goals and ideas as well as intertwining with the energies of all the other people and aspects in your life, including your culture and time and the consciousness you are immersed in. This is why it is necessary to sense and feel into the possibilities surrounding you and why there can be so many possibilities.

We do hope individuals can take strength from accepting that there is meaning in all elements of life, including disruption. Learn to anchor into the part of yourself that is connected with All There Is, with the Source, and know you will again find the avenue of your spiritual expression. Remember, you can express the spiritual essence of the self without having specific spiritual practices. This is very important.

> **The idea is not to make up or direct**
> **your reality in specific ways,**
> **but rather, to consistently open your**
> **awareness to all the directions before you.**

Creating one's life is not simply working with the present conscious intent. Again, think of it as a vast connecting force of many elements and that the individual's quest is to increase the awareness and sensitivity to these elements, but not to ever fully direct every moment from the conscious mind. As we have said at other times, the conscious mind is a wonderful tool, but it is limited.

Thus, even if one were able to totally control every aspect of life, it would be a sad thing to do this with the limitations of the conscious mind – which, no matter how educated or expanded, it cannot, by virtue of its mechanism, be nearly as full and rich as the Inner Awareness and Expanded Awareness. One must resist becoming too goal directed or thinking there will be an end time; thinking there will be a full awareness, a super nova of consciousness, and then you will be there. Rather, view life as a continuing blossoming. You must accept the validity of each choice.

All the turnings and choices will take you to
the center of the maze and on to the exit.
In the grand scheme it matters not what path,
but to travel on a path.

Your spiritual awareness of the wholeness of all things can lead you nowhere but to an understanding that the wholeness and correctness of all things very often can mean what seems to be negative. On the personal level, death is a sad thing and yet it is accepted as part of your nature. Many of you may know how an individual's apparently untimely, tragic death releases a torrent of changes in many of the people and situations around that person. One thinks, 'But why did that small child have to die?' And yet you can see how that circumstance created so much. This is part of the continuing paradox of your life.

The idea again, is that your individual wisdom, your feelings, your connection, is somehow valid. It is to know that your note in the symphony has an effect and may indeed create the ideals that you hold. Indeed, the ideals you hold may be the ones that will bring your version of balance and harmony. But it would be too simple for us to simply tell you that there will be a definite outcome reflecting everyone's image of peace and love. There are many people who do not use or view those terms in the same way. But if you get too caught up in these final images and outcomes, your present, this moment, becomes lost.

Trust the inner wisdom –
not only for personal development,
but also to direct energies into the world.

Sense where your life is going. Sense where your society is going. Trust the inner wisdom; yes, trust the inner wisdom not just for your own personal psychological development, but also for ways to direct these energies into the world. Many of you may choose to be active. Others may choose: 'I will live my life by these principles I hold dear and that will reverberate through the world.'

Life does not 'get there.' Life is motion.

The only caution is you must hold the acceptance that you can set the direction, but you cannot totally predict and control the outcome. The webs of energy hold an integrity of their own, linking you in ways not perceived by the conscious self. Also, the outcome for the greater good may not be as you imagine it. This concept can overwhelm, so it all must be treated lightly. There are certain degrees of acceptance that you must come to, and from there, change can occur. Life does not 'get there'. Life is motion.

It does not help to judge yourself
if you have made what seems a wrong turning.
It is simply the choice you made, and you only need
to see where it has brought you.

We should like to discuss the power of accountability and responsibility in one's life. Often this concept is not used to uplift, to make one feel more in control or able to direct life, to feel power. These words are used to mean that one is responsible, that one is accountable, and how each individual has created every aspect of the individual life. Thus, the idea of accountability and responsibility often leads to feelings generated as guilt.

As we have said, responsibility can be read as respond-ability, the ability to respond. You see, that is very different than great guilt upon your shoulders, fear of wrong choices and misinformation, which is how responsibility is often viewed in your society. Some who begin to explore the spiritual side have also taken the view that one is at conscious fault for everything you feel is untoward or negative that comes into your life. This approach can be counter-productive.

Remember, there is not only one response. Again, it does not help to judge yourself if you have made what seems a wrong turning. It is helpful to use discernment. It is simply the choice you made, and you only need to see where it has brought you. All the turnings and choices will take you to the center of the maze, to the exit. In the grand scheme it matters not what path, but to follow a path. You must accept the validity of each choice. Do not berate yourself with 'Why have I created this?' Exploring unexamined feelings and patterns may help you discover the basis for a choice that seems less satisfying. At other times, proceed from accepting that which has occurred and consider, 'However this has been created, I can find a way to learn from this, to see something new, for this very choice to serve me.' What you feel are wrong steps, often are the very ones that take you to a new place or a journey you could not have imagined.

SPIRITUAL PIONEERS

Living the spiritual path is staying attuned to the
inner energies and to the alignment of energy.
Very often this alignment leads individuals to be in conflict
with some of the acceptable social mores of their time.
These are the individuals who are able to
fashion their own niche – the spiritual pioneers.

We would like to talk on the challenge that occurs when expressing what is called 'the spiritual path' takes you outside of the structure of society. To be clear, the spiritual path is not to be confused with spiritual expression. In our view, spiritual practices such as religion, dietary regimens such as vegetarianism, physical practices such as yoga, are all outward expressions of the inner dynamic. It is not inherent that such outward expressions lead you to spiritual understanding and awareness. Rather, these are expressions in outward form of the inner self. Often you have explored these spiritual practices to come into a concrete conscious conceptualization of inherent principles within you, which are then demonstrated through such spiritual practices.

Seeing yourself as the pioneer is a much more positive image than seeing yourself as the outsider. For those of you who somehow feel not at ease, who somehow feel really not connected with people or situations, use the model of yourself as explorer and pioneer. Use this model to allow yourself to see where you may lead yourself.

It is difficult to be pioneers.
But, many of you are.

Following one's own alignment does not necessarily mean it is your responsibility or path to bring others into that alignment. Another element that needs balancing by the pioneer is that some people will come into alignment with you and others will experience you as quite jarring and disturbing. You may not be able to reach them, to align with them.

Many of you are beginning to come
into conscious awareness that you
relate to this world and your own society differently –
differently than many people you know,
differently than what you know historically.

The forms of relating are growing. They are not here yet, these new ways of relating, and for some of you, you are in the difficult in-between state, the hybrid stage. We wish to encourage you to allow yourselves to come into awareness that what you create, how you feel about someone, how you relate to someone, may be fully appropriate. You may find that you have no model to reflect on.

We are not underestimating at all the difficulty of relating within a society differently than the society's main structure. Let us encourage you to allow yourself to conceptualize, to allow yourself to see in your mind, new and different ways of relating to each other. Do not condemn yourselves. Do not limit yourselves. Do not judge yourselves. Know that you are a pioneer. And although you may be unique, you are not alone either. There are many of you having the same struggle.

> **The ego discipline we recommend is
> to listen to the Inner Awareness.**

We do not align ourselves strongly with certain ideas about ego discipline and spiritual teaching. We offer a somewhat different approach. The discipline we suggest does not come from the ego. We feel disciplining the ego is not what is needed. Rather, the ego consciousness needs nurturing and educating, assistance in expanding its parameters.

The discipline we recommend is to listen to the Inner Awareness, giving yourself moments to allow the information that is fully yours to come into your conscious mind. Thus, the actions you take, the forms you create, are fully informed from far-reaching levels of your awareness. This is the discipline we are seeking and this discipline has its own natural flow of timing. It is very easy to work with this kind of approach with time commitments. It becomes a natural progression and again, we are talking about integration.

We see individuals as having available full information and knowledge to be spiritual individuals. As you integrate and create your expression of spiritual principles, you will integrate those principles as an integral part of all aspects of your life; which is our main focus. This is not to say that you will not take many aspects from extant systems, and that at certain times in your life you will be very faithful in enacting these principles or rules or ideas as set down. We are not judging these other systems, but in our view, there are many people on who are ready to begin the next step where the student truly becomes self-educated. The systems and the information, including information such as we are presenting, are all tools to be used by the individual. Therefore, there is no one outcome; there are many expressions.

> Your interaction with this realm,
> this Earth matrix, this life aspect,
> is a deep commitment.

We begin with the idea that each of you in a state of full consciousness, fuller than you can simply imagine, chose to express yourself as a physical being in this timing and physical place. This is an empowerment concept. We do not say this to make you feel overwhelmed by the enormity of responsibility. Although you may not be able to actualize full understanding and mastery of how this choice is made or why, the true understanding and knowledge that this is chosen should be an element of security, of connection with the inner being, and therefore it should be empowering.

You have chosen this commitment, have chosen this present. Your interaction with this realm, this Earth matrix, this life aspect, is a deep commitment. We remind you again of the idea of integration. As you try to expand your conscious awareness of this realm to include other realms or awareness, the challenge is to allow yourself a broad perspective and then intertwine this perspective into your active living. Simply releasing yourself into experiencing and not being able to allow yourself to bring your experience and awareness into form and action within your daily reality would be a sad occurrence.

Life in form is not a lesser aspect of being.

We are very distressed that this is an extensively held belief on the planet. There is the idea of the earth plane as a reality of punishment, retribution, and a need to learn one's lessons. We are fond of reminding people that for us to continue our spiritual growth and development, we have had to make use of another's dense physical form. Working within form is a method of choice. Life in the earth reality is an option, an alternative in a great realm of possibilities.

The idea that this reality is of less value, more mundane in a negative way, is also prevalent. We offer the idea that there is great validity in every aspect of living. We remind you that there are ways to express Spirit in this form and action which are unique. We wish you would allow yourself to perceive this present reality as a vital opportunity of existence. This earth is your committed place. Whatever your soul roots, your soul travels, your soul groupings, the commitment in action, the commitment for the form to create, is on this planet. Experience a further awareness of this Earth matrix, this place of your commitment. Rooting in the committed place always creates a foundation for the further explorations.

ON SPIRITUAL SELF–RESPECT

We see a time of a cooperative working,
of an effort to increase awareness
and receptivity on many levels.
You must begin by having the idea of
spiritual self-respect.

We honor those of you who allow yourselves exploration and connection with such as us. We remind you that we offer a perspective, not the ultimate truth. We are not the authority. All we share is to be considered with discernment. We are interested in stimulating your ability to link with your own Core Essence of awareness. And with such awareness, you can consider and weigh that which we share from our perspective.

Consider as well the premise of *exchange* between realms. Respect that beings such as us may offer an expanded view, but do not couple this with ideas of your realm as being less. We would like to encourage the idea of an interactive cooperative relationship between realms or levels of awareness.

We see very strongly individuals garnering more spiritual respect for themselves. You have something to offer. It is understood that when one studies with a teacher, in some way, even if unknown by the student, the student serves the teacher as well. We suggest you embrace this idea. To be totally in awe of energy systems outside of your reality will no longer serve in the way it has at other times. This is not a time needing worship or deification of these energies. We see a time of a hand-in-hand, cooperative working effort to increase awareness and receptivity on many levels. You must begin by having the idea of spiritual self-respect.

Will you consider that in your inner wisdom, in that inner core spark connected to All There Is, there is knowledge and awareness and wisdom yet untapped by you? You have reserves of awareness not present in your conscious mind. Be prepared to permit yourself to honor your potential, in the very least. Further, see yourself as one who is willing not only to receive, but who honors an aspect of reciprocation, even though it may not be in a conscious or deliberate way. Many individuals who do permit interaction with other levels soon come to an inner-knowing that their connection is serving and contributing to the greater well-being of other levels, even if they cannot define or give definite examples.

> Living your life integrated with
> your spiritual perspective is a
> true communication of spiritual energy.

It is quite exhilarating to think of spirituality being expressed through the individual, slight variations that each person can bring to this planet. Envision the power of all those vibrations. Envision the power of all those individuals attuned to their inner core, integrating their own unique expression and understanding. Envision the power as they send out into their world and the universe their attuned vibrations and energy. It is truly powerful and uplifting. The expression of spirituality which is custom-made by an individual for that individual is more powerful than any off-the-rack suit.

Remember, it is not necessary for spiritual energy to be communicated as words defining or explaining spirituality. You as artist or musician, you as teacher or clerk, will find that living your life integrated with your spiritual perspective is a true communication of spiritual energy.

Realize there are layers, moving patterns,
realms of connectedness and understanding –
not statically existing, but in motion.
This motion is flowing with vitality
and you are part of this Multiverse.
Live your life with complexity.
Know that each thing is never just as it seems.

CHAPTER FOUR

AXIOMS OF AWARENESS

INTEGRATION

A world where the interconnection of all things –
in a spiritual vein, in a physical vein –
is rekindled, and such interconnection
is a part of everything.

Our goal is to bring integration of the spiritual awareness within your day to day reality. Integration is not a static state. It is a flow that moves in a natural pace. As an example, the Inner Awareness brings to a person an idea that someone is coming to visit and will soon be arriving at the door. The Inner Awareness flows and an integrated person allows the sense of the Inner Awareness to touch into their conscious mind, and an integrated person does not dismiss it. An integrated person will take the moment to listen within and allow action to flow, such as going to greet the visitor.

The Expanded Awareness also works in the same flow. If you are calling to your life a certain desire, such as a job application, you send out the energy. The Expanded Awareness is quite capable of reaching out and bringing in the information needed. Through integration with the Inner Awareness, the conscious mind listens and takes action.

Spirituality that is not brought into form and action, particularly for those of you who have chosen to be a part of form and action, is a very sad occurrence. It is wasteful and a frustrating way to live. We emphasize the premise of a spirituality that becomes an integral part of your being. This is a spirituality you use in all ways, naturally and flowingly. You are not always operating from Inner Awareness; you are not always operating from Expanded Awareness.

One moves and flows through levels of awareness – conscious, inner, expanded – as the need fits. An integrated person expands the parameters of the conscious mind to allow the conscious mind to take what it receives from the inner levels, understand it, and then allow the awareness to come into form.

> Hold the idea of the spiritual path integrated
> within any chosen work, any chosen path.

Recognizing the ability to be separate, and yet not to be destroyed, is an integral part of moving into integration. It is a stepping stone for the conscious mind to accept that separation does not necessarily lead to disintegration or death – death of the personality, death of patterns or abilities. Thus, each of you is able to come to a conscious realization of your ability to fit within and without the various segments of your culture that you move through.

Can we encourage you to realize that you don't have to work on everything? Here we are at odds with the society, but we are taking a long view. We wish to bring the idea of the spiritual path into an integration with any chosen work, any chosen path, a naturalness that is simply part and parcel of the expression of being.

There is such potential of all sorts of expression from one being.

For some of you the path of self-awareness and spiritual discovery is your central focus. On the whole, this is positive. Yet, we see something out of balance here. We see other channels of your life being untapped or neglected: creativity, music, relationships. In creativity and other ways you are limiting the time you give to express yourself in these outlets. You are judging that you do not have time. You are judging that other outlets are not as important as your soul searching, as your spiritual quest. Spirituality is then being put in a separate niche, in a separate focus. Spirituality is not becoming part and parcel of your life. Spirituality is not becoming integrated into your life.

We are certainly not saying that you must give up conscious understanding and expansion of spirituality as your main focus. We encourage you to not have too narrow or rigid a focus. Allow yourselves all the other elements in life. We feel there can be too much rigid identification of the self as a spiritual being, with a limited definition of what being spiritual means. You observe these limiting patterns in other individuals: the friend who is the lawyer who can only speak of law. The person who becomes totally focused on money. People are still very bound up by the images of spirituality, such as that one who is spiritual is mostly not sexual, eats only certain healthy foods, is very gentle at all times, never tells jokes. You are all so many things and there is such potential here of all sorts of expressions from one being. An expanded individual, a full individual, is truly a spiritual individual. Embrace the wholistic view in all things, including your spiritual identity.

Picture, if you will, people who have a spiritual focus, who are engaged in being aware and sensitive and responding to themselves, but who are also full people who laugh, make merry, who have good times. Picture people who are creative, who appreciate the arts, who are kind, who have pets, etc. This would be a very fully expressive world. We want to encourage nurturing of a world where the interconnection of all things is rekindled and is recognized a part of everything.

> You are all bearing energy and
> light and awareness and openness.

Do not ever underestimate how one individual can affect the world at large. Each of you has affected many people in ways you do not realize. You are all bearing energy and light and awareness and openness. You will begin to notice that it is hard to maintain integration if all change and learning must come through catharsis or through dramatic upheaval. Too many individuals cast aside where they have been as they embrace where they are now or look to where they are going. You can pass from an intense stage of focus and hold an element of some program or process within you. This is synthesizing your own belief structure through integration, rather than casting aside one element and passionately embracing another.

We try to encourage people to get away from the idea of what has been called the spiritual 'high', the cathartic experience, the 'ah-ha!' These states are wonderful, and for many allow a major change. But if you create the expectation that all awareness must come in this format, you can create a difficult life for yourself. And you are missing the subtleness of other ways of relating.

You are not gaining perfection.
You are bringing it to your conscious awareness.
The perfection IS.
The crystal of perfection is present
in every one of you, in all living things.

When one strives to be expanded at all times and acting in a 'spiritual' manner, you can lose sight of what is already present. The success of the present moment is *not* experienced. Instead, being successful, feeling 'together,' being *whole*, is what only the future holds for you; it is seeing as what you are *becoming*. Yet, if only the *future* holds the whole person, who is now present? Is it the imperfect person, the mediocre person or the almost-there-but-not-quite person? This is the danger and difficulty with over-focusing on striving to evolve and holding specific images of your evolution and growth.

Consider yourself instead as a beautiful, clear, perfectly formed natural crystal. What you are doing with this crystal is not making it more perfect. You understand it, finding out all the things you can do with it. Therefore, the approach is, 'I am this perfect being and I am going to explore all the ways I can bring that perfection into my awareness.' You are not gaining perfection. You are bringing it to your conscious awareness. The perfection IS. The crystal is present in every one of you, in all living things.

THE LONG HAUL

**We are looking forward to seeing individuals
who integrate spiritual expression
into their lives on a daily basis for all of their lives.**

We are very concerned with what we call the 'long haul' – the idea that people develop awareness of their spiritual self in a way that is integrated with all the other choices in their life. This development is over time and is consistent, but need not be constant. The long haul is to live life as it is. It is not to set your life into a system, but to let you see and explore systems which come into your life. It is evolution.

When you find your inner sense directing you in a way that your conscious mind is resisting and your society and culture is perhaps not supporting you – stop! Sense. Explore your own history. Believe in your Innate Wisdom and let it guide you and help you choose what you need to do to bring learning into conscious awareness. Use the long view to explore ideas and images from other times, places, cultures of your reality. Consider the idea that there is no singular for-all-time approach to belief systems.

If you find yourself moving into judgment and easily assigning this judgment as coming from Creator energy, you should be cautioned. Look again with the long view at your own history and see how what is acceptable now was not acceptable a short time ago. This does not mean one casts aside moral structure. It means you must be cautious in making these structures and beliefs more rigidly defined and more powerful than they are. The fact that things are mutable, that things can change - in your thoughts, in your beliefs, in your life - does not mean life is without internal meaning. It means, rather, that there are levels, shades, and variations of meaning. Meanings flow and move and change. Hold the image, the icon of change as evolving, growing, and blossoming - all of which are totally natural processes.

We are looking forward to seeing individuals who integrate spiritual expression into their lives on a daily, everyday basis for all of their lives. Do not think of the mundane as simply 'holding time' or simply passing time away in-between each high point, in-between the 'important' aspects of life. We are hoping all of you in your long and full lives, will find a way, perhaps with an assist from our sharing, to expand yourselves and your awareness in a regular, easy and natural manner. We hope that you can consistently become sensitive to far more than your physical body.

ACCOUNTABILITY

Experience empowerment through understanding
the nature of yourself and choose a willingness
to be accountable for and responsible to
the nature of yourself and the actions you bring.

As people move along the path of discovering their own nature, choosing consciously to explore spirituality or to study the nature of reality, it is then the individual's responsibility to choose accountability. How many of you feel misunderstood? How many of you feel, 'I can't connect with anyone who really knows where I'm coming from, who really feels me?' You feel frustration with your friends, with your partners, with your lovers. A strong myth in your society is that you will find the perfect match. Some of you use the term soul mate. Others, less mystical, simply look for someone who will accept you as you are. Unconditional love is a phrase that is used very often.

We would like to offer another perspective for you to consider. As you come to understanding of yourself, seeing through your own experiences how you can perceive at times a broader view, that you can sense and learn to follow those senses and have them proved valid; that you are quite comfortable, as an example, thinking of the existence of other realities or other realms, we ask you to acknowledge that you must use your nature and your understanding of that nature in a way that truly communicates. When you come to an understanding that an element of you is unique, understand that this uniqueness is often an extraordinary gift, but a gift you must be accountable to.

It is not the task of others to learn quickly enough to match you. It is not the task of others to open their energies so they can feel and sense you accurately. How many are waiting for that? It must not be that your uniqueness brings responsibility unto others to acknowledge or cope with these differences. It is you who are exploring expanded sensing abilities. It is you who must embrace the accountability of dealing with modulation, explanation, and finding support for the understanding of your perspective. This willingness to be accountable to how others experience you is not a weight of responsibility in a negative fashion. It gives you the key to facilitate communication, real extension and snaring of yourself. It is your task because you have chosen this kind of conscious awareness exploration. It is your task to learn modulation, balancing and true communication.

When the feedback you continue to get is that you are overwhelming, that you are too odd, that you 'make me uncomfortable,' perhaps you could think – instead of feeling, 'I must separate from this person' or 'This person just doesn't know what I'm all about' – that perhaps they are sharing with you a true view, a true perspective. Perhaps it is time for you to consider, 'Am I, out there sharing and presenting, really communicating and linking, as I feel I am? Or rather, am I energy-wise, concept-wise, and language-wise truly overwhelming?'

Allow yourself to come into clear recognition of the nature of your being. Allow yourself to support yourself, understand and accept yourself. You might find you are then willing to and able to understand that when another person cannot fully accept you or participate with you as you wish, it may mean not a rejection, but simply an energy inability to participate with you in your full self.

You will see it is not giving up of yourself or compromise in any negative way, when you experiment with the ideas of subtlety and modulation. It is, instead, really a tool you are willing to use for true communication and exchange. When we talk of modulation or modification, we find that people become very closed and private. The idea of expansion and openness is a lovely ideal when it serves, when it is harmonious. But it is not a singular element that must be presented in a singular note at all times.

We encourage you to consider looking again at the shadings, the subtleties, the tonalities of relating.

When a person feels overwhelmed by your energy, instead of turning to anger or separation, experiment with taking a moment to pull in that overwhelming energy. Experiment with taking a moment to not use the terms that you are comfortable with and find other words, another way of communicating and speaking that the other person can truly comprehend and understand. This kind of modulation is not compromising yourself. It is a reflection of accepting and understanding the nature of yourself. It will give you a true tool for communicating, for sharing.

Now people do this all the time and do not feel compromised. When you talk to a small child, even if you very much hold the ideal that you won't talk 'down' to the child, you still have to in some ways alter your vocabulary. Some people if they are very tall, even go down to the child's height. If you were from another culture and were communicating, you would use clear words. You would use gestures. You wouldn't continue to expect the other people to immediately accept you in any expression that you wanted to give. Even when you are dealing with those you consider your compatriots, at times you still need to modulate the energy exchange.

When you hear someone say you are 'too intense,' they may not at all be saying 'go away.' They can be trying to say, 'Help me communicate with you.' It seems a lot of people are missing the idea that perhaps they *are* too intense. Perhaps you have expanded your way of viewing things, perhaps you've expanded literally the ability to exchange energy and now you are abruptly colliding with other people's energy systems, perhaps including a vocabulary or an expectation they cannot understand, let alone meet. Embrace accountability. Accountability can act as a great balancing; a fine integrator, rather than a great burden of self-talk, as in 'I am responsible, I have to handle it all, or It's up to me!'

Understand accountability and responsibility
to the self as a gift you embrace for yourself.

When another person consistently does not understand, it may simply be that they do *not* understand. It may be that you are speaking with energies that say more than they can comprehend in words. The energy reaches them before the words you speak do, and they literally do not hear the words. If it happens again and again, accept that perhaps you need to find another way to communicate. Less intense. Different words. Writing. Whatever it would be.

If it is your goal to communicate and share of yourself, finding ways to communicate effectively and learning to pull in your energy when necessary will give you a true foundation of relating. In this way, you are not left feeling rejected or misunderstood, passively accepting that no one can perceive you correctly. You are, instead, willing to step into the active mode of trying to truly *communicate*; offering yourself and participating in the exchange.

Modulation does not mean lessening or diminishing.

It doesn't mean you are being hypocritical. It doesn't mean you are hiding, that you are undercover. Do not confuse the societal idea and ideal that every person should be totally open (which is an ideal of your time and place, not of all cultures) with the idea that you should be open to awareness of yourself; respecting and

55

honoring the awareness levels and perception levels of others. If the idea is to share and communicate, to participate together, then without condescension, without arrogance, one allows acceptance and understands that the more expansive a person is the more that person holds the responsibility for and ability of communication.

Now it may be people still will find you overwhelming and will separate from you, but we also offer the thought that some people, when you consciously choose modulation and subtlety, will be able to link with you. When you've really made a link, when you have permitted someone to come into your energy system, when you've found the words that will help them conceptualize what you want to share, you will discover many opportunities for intensity and the other person will be able to extend their intensity and share and participate with yours. Respect yourselves as wise beings who are consciously choosing expansion and, in that respect, we also remind you of the mantle of responsibility and accountability we sincerely hope you are willing to shoulder.

There is no singular way to come into the fullness of your awareness.

Accountability is present for yourself. Each of you needs to be more compassionate, more forgiving, more loving to yourself. Being a hard task master will eventually 'burn you out'; exploring will become hard and difficult and you will wish to pull away from the focus of the spiritual view. This is why we so much encourage lightness and a non-judgmental, forgiving approach to oneself. We hope you would be able to live your life in a blossoming, gentle, natural exploration of self. Can you see that if you are judging every moment, every choice, chastising yourself for doing the wrong things, you will eventually give up your quest?

Often the spiritual quest becomes a time of your life. We would like to forestall this by our encouragement of the long haul. Integrating spirituality in your life can be a natural part of living, like breathing. Already it is part of you. Spirituality is not meant to correct you. Spirituality is not to make a negative become good. You see, you *are* good. Each of you. The inner spark is inherently good. You are all directing yourselves with inherent goodness. Spirituality lets you discover again and again this inherent goodness.

> Embrace respond-ability to yourselves with
> a light, gentle, compassionate, forgiving manner.

Those things in yourself you are not so pleased with, can we recommend that you look at them again? How are they serving you? When you find you are trying too hard with little success, do not embrace it as a task that must be bulldozed through. Could you consider instead, is it a task that, perhaps, doesn't really need your focus? It is not wrong to choose the easier approach. This may seem to be in conflict with some other approaches in which great discipline, deprivation, and the like are required. If that is what appeals to you, certainly, you will use that discipline to your fullest advantage. Yet, a specifically disciplined approach is not the only way.

Awareness is a moving thing, an ongoing part of life.

There is no singular way to come into the fullness of your awareness. You may evolve many ways of working with awareness. We remind you also that awareness is a continuum. Awareness is a moving thing. The fullness will not come and be achieved and then sit there with you. It will be part of life.

HONORING THE SELF

To honor yourself is simply to acknowledge
a positive action, a loving spirit.
It is acknowledgement of a talent,
an achievement, one's integrity.

We invite you, encourage you, and remind you to honor yourselves. Honoring is a combination of recognition and respect, of paying attention and giving credit where credit is due. It can, for many of you, naturally expand into real feelings of integration and connectedness and self-love. But honoring is a first step that even individuals who are frightened and vulnerable within, who are uncomfortable with the idea of their perfection, can take. You begin by, for yourself, to yourself, just making a statement of 'Yes, I am like that.' 'Yes, I gave my best.' 'Yes, I tried.' 'Yes, I did do that.' Doing this in the most minimal way does not create a minimal action. Rather, you create large, broad strokes of action on planes outside your recognition. So, each minimal time you honor yourself by taking one moment to acknowledge and respect one small element or action, there are great shifts. As you move into it more and more consistently, feeling the actions grow and flow, you begin to experience honoring of self and experience comfort levels within your being. You begin to experience true self-assurance. This assurance may not apply to all of your actions, for you may still do things you are not yet assured of. But, you will come to know a kind of self-assurance for yourself simply about yourself.

It is important for you to always -
in balance and harmony, not in egotism -
take the moment to feel that power
and wisdom within the self.

When you have accepted and taken and moved with new knowledge and awareness, take the moment please, the important moment, to honor yourself. Take the moment to look at your own courageousness and your own expansion. Allow yourself to see how you have accepted and permitted opening of the self. Use such honoring to hold the power to the self, from the self, through the self. You are tapping into energies. You are allowing receptivity and you are the pivotal bringer about of the change. We are all really working together and it is important for you to always, in balance and harmony without egotism, take the moment to feel that power and wisdom within the self.

We are very much looking forward to your experiencing and honoring for yourself your own moments of excellence. You may never say it to another person or you may grow comfortable with sharing your knowledge of your strengths. But, as you feel and experience your own value, you will find yourself getting much more feedback from the outside world. What will have shifted is your permitting of the feedback and by honoring the self it more clearly allows others to receive your energy of self-worth. They feel you and your excellence more clearly and reflect it back to you. Then, when you have periods of doubts or confusion, you can touch and use your own history to support yourself, to demonstrate to yourself how there can be another turn in the road.

This creates anchoring so, when the outside world crashes in, when other people buffet you, you are not completely thrown off. You regain your balance. Balancing is active. Balancing comes easier because you honor yourself and you have the ability to touch into that honoring. Honoring is, of course, not to be used in a negative sense. It is not conceit. Negativity comes from extremes and from manipulation. An important key to opening pathways – physical pathways, energy pathways – of receptivity, wherein you may experience the influx of harmony and balancing energy, is honoring yourself.

> Be thankful to yourself for your growth,
> for the challenges you have met,
> for the choices you have brought to yourself.
> You are your own teachers.

You teach yourself through the fullness of you, which you have the ability to touch into. You teach yourself, as well, through the conscious, present reality of you. We do not want you to hold the idea that you are only a perfect being when you are connected with that which is greater than the being you are in this moment.

Each individual is an important note in the symphony.
Each life expression is an essential note in the symphony.

We encourage you to accept the idea of the validation of the all of you. This present energy of your being is the focus of your attention and spiritual expression and the connection with All There Is right now. This reality is not simply passing time on the way to a greater existence or just a part of many other parts. This reality is a unique, valued, important, specific energy expression giving balance and wholeness to all the other parts of yourself. The conscious world you are in now is the reality of your delight. It is the reality of your love.

Live life with a willingness to look at
things again and again in a different way.
This is growth. This is balance.
This is harmony. This is living at the fullest.

Live life with fullness, with exploration, with consistent attempts at understanding. Live life with acknowledgement that you are somehow interacting with more than you can think of. Live life where you try to feel the connections, where you allow and permit information to be received. Live life with a willingness to look at things again and again in a different way. This is growth. This is the spiritual expression. This is the highest service, the highest impulse. This is balance. This is harmony. This is living at the fullest.

> There are gifts within you.
> Some you are beginning to discover.
> Some you are going to rediscover.

We also want to remind each of you that you are all gifted. Some gifts you have yet to see - they are waiting for you. We want you to think on the idea that you are special, you are important, and yet, you also have the abilities to help give to others the awareness of their specialness, their importance, their note in the symphony.

You see, acknowledging your specialness never means you must then be separate. This is a fear present with many of you that if you are really a special person, you are going to be separated or separate from others. There is the fear that you must never admit your specialness, for others may feel judged by you and will separate from you. The idea of the unique and special note in the symphony serves because it reminds you of the value of each thing, even if you cannot see it separately in and of itself.

> Holding respect and value for the essence of each being is honoring the self. One who honors the unique note in the symphony does not move into judgment of the self or others. Thus, honoring the self also serves as a tool of balance.

ALLOWING & PERMITTING

When you are balancing the co-creation of reality,
you are allowing and permitting.

Allowing and permitting are elements of receptivity and awareness. You set directions. You set goals. You orient yourself toward the goals. You take the action towards the goals. But the balancing aspect, the part that keeps the integrity of the greater whole, is being willing to release the expected outcome, and therefore allow yourself to enter into outcomes that become clear to you as they evolve. These outcomes may not be those you had consciously planned.

You notice we say willing to, which means you need not always release the expected outcome. The expected outcome may come to pass exactly as you imagined it. The balancing is in the willingness to keep the awareness and receptiveness open to the other currents. It is important for you to let yourself have those levels, even if it is uncomfortable, and you can sense levels of anxiety or ambivalence. Let yourself come into alignment. Don't try to push it or over-program it. Alignment is a moving thing. Alignment is seen in the final fit, in the resolution.

Sometimes alignment occurs cathartically. Other times alignment comes through fitting and refitting. There can be times of depression and stress. There can be times of anxiety, ambivalence and fear. All these things are indications of movement and action.

63

Allow such times. Permit them. Embrace them as signs of co-creation occurring. Begin to explore allowing and permitting. State your intent that you will be receptive and that your conscious mind will recognize the awareness or information you have received. Perhaps you will create a quiet time, a meditative time to allow this information to come to awareness. But it also can be that you will be doing the dishes and awareness – thoughts, words, visions, knowledge of a whole point – will pop into your mind. These are ways that communications through the awareness levels are felt. You must permit an expanded view in your conscious mind, which accepts that you can receive information or communication from levels other than conscious thought.

Once the dialogue has been established with the inner levels, the delicate part is to simply accept what you receive of its own accord and be willing to move with it, rather than trying to create consciously how you will receive and what the information will be. There is nothing wrong in stating what you feel you want to know. It is only when you try to force or stringently direct how the information will be presented or received that you can interfere with the natural flow of awareness. People ask questions wanting the answer they want and they are very unreceptive when the answer is not as they desire. This can close off communication. Allow the experiences to be as they are. Do not rush to judge them. Do not rush to formulate concrete images of what it must mean.

The evolution of a new pattern will happen in its own time.

Let go of the idea of forcing patterns in your life to change. You need to allow thought patterns to change. The idea is to bring the elements of awareness you have gathered through the inner processes to your conscious thoughts. This puts them into a conscious recognition level, so when you find yourself acting in an old pattern, you recognize it. This recognition already has altered the pattern of behavior. You cannot continue to act as you had in the past. Change is occurring. The point is, do not try to *stop* an old pattern. Let another pattern *evolve* from the old.

If you cannot feel comfortable saying, 'I'm not going to do that any longer,' then don't say it! Perhaps you are more comfortable saying, 'I'm going to try this.' If the old pattern is still pulling you, work with it. The goal is to have assimilation, an integration of the existing patterns toward the new ideal. You are using the understanding you have garnered through your Inner Awareness to permit the new patterns to begin evolving.

New ways of relating feel awkward at first. They don't seem to work, but in time, they will. Fighting the natural flow of growth uses a lot of energy unproductively. Unfortunately, its the same kind of energy as worry – it feels like you're doing something, but actually you're not, because the evolution of the new patterns, the outcome, is still going to happen in its own time.

Evolution is not always a smooth flow. There is movement: ups and downs, 'two steps forward, one step back.' All such terms are reflections of the reality of how energy works. Positive outcomes, positive change can come in ways that might feel uncomfortable to you. It may be that there is awareness and information that may feel distressing or uncomfortable when you receive them.

WORKING WITH ALLOWING AND PERMITTING

Allowing and permitting can be used in many situations. For example, the question is asked, 'We have a meeting at my son's school at the end of the month, with my son's teacher and several other people and we're feeling rather apprehensive.'

We suggest before the meeting you would allow yourself to visualize or think of the idea of receptivity, of unity, of a linking, between all the participants, all the elements involved. Hold the idea that the outcome will be of a positive nature. Hold the idea that it is needful for all that will be shared to be shared. Say to yourself, 'I am going to be receptive to information I need to hear for my son.' Ask that all the information you need begin to flow to you. Ask that you be receptive to opportunities and understandings that may come to you. See if you can put aside fears of overwhelming accountabilities and responsibilities you may have. Set aside, if you can, the psychological element and just allow the information element.

Also, give yourselves permission to listen and not take action at that time. If you are called upon to take immediate action, you have the right to say, 'We really must consider all of this. We feel your concern and were going to consider it all and we'll talk to you tomorrow.' Giving yourself this permission will help you to not react through fear and emotion. Instead, you will permit yourself to hear the actual concrete information. If you then disagree or want to re-evaluate, etc., you will be able to do that in your own realm, in your own privacy. You will then be able to *respond*, not react.

You create the opportunity to consider information away from the stress situation by planning your course of allowing and permitting beforehand. You know you are going to say, 'We cannot tell you right now what action we will take. We must have time to consider.' You need to think of this beforehand, because the situation may be that the other people will want your immediate response to their urgency. Thus, what you will do is honor the validity of their feelings. 'Yes, we see you feel this strongly. We are going to respond, but we must have time to consider.' This way you do not also have to be concerned with saying the 'right thing', the correct thing.

A key to growth is the phrase, 'I realized'.

Realization is when you allow and permit awareness to come clear. It is coupled with thinking and considering, but 'thinking' by itself can keep the control in the more narrow realm of the conscious

67

mind. When you permit conscious exploration of ideas, permission to experience another perspective is being created.

ALIGNMENT

**Respect the currents of energy in the same way
you would work with currents in nature.**

There is meaning in life and each day has a meaning. Growth is incremental. We remind you of the importance of feeling the alignments in your life. Even if you cannot perceive them and understand them as they occur, if you can consider the idea that there is meaning, that alignments are possible, perhaps you can use such an idea – which we consider a reality, but we ask you only to consider as an idea – to sustain yourself.

You can use retrospect as a tool.

Retrospect occurs when certain elements have come into alignment and the conscious mind can then recognize and perceive the pattern of things falling into place, and you come to conscious understanding. When you cannot get information, when it is all confused and a jumble, in our perspective it is *literally* confused and a jumble. The energy is moving, flowing, tumbling, and very often the difficulty comes from trying to pursue and anchor energy that is in such turmoil. When you step back and simply acknowledge that this confusion is present, you often find that when you remove your energy from trying to control the situation, the other energy, in and of itself, comes into an alignment.

Aligned energy is energy you can identify, recognize, and connect with. This is the natural phenomenon of what thoughts, emotions, feelings, and actions are. They are energy patterns which, in time, your own science will be able to identify and see. We do not mean this in a mystifying manner. What you describe in emotional terms as a confused energy, a 'nothing working' kind of energy, to us, is an accurate description of the process.

You will find, the more you are willing to work with the energies you perceive, the easier you will find choices, actions, decisions are to make. You all have seen it in your own lives. When you try to force the issue, there is a time it can work and a time it cannot. Retrospectively, you will probably notice the time you stepped back from active pursuit and then the action went forward. You let go and the outcome came to you. Think of it as working with currents, like air currents or water currents. Respect the currents of energy in the same way you would work with currents in nature.

OPTIONS & CHOICES

*These aspects remind you that life is
a mutable, moveable, flexible experience.*

You can have certain structures and patterns that support you. But always hold in mind that it is a *mutable* structure supporting you. It is not walls. It is not permanent. It is not locked doors. You can always find other ways to relate to a situation. Find other ways to be. You can turn around a situation that seems to be inexorably creeping along a certain way. It may be an easy task. It may be a difficult one. But as energy flows and changes, all things can flow and change.

> It is not that you are going to achieve balance.
> It is that you are going to be balanc*ing*.

Motion is the by-word of growth and change. Sometimes you will not feel the motion. Sometimes change is not viable, but it is available. It can evolve. Sometimes you cannot choose it in one moment, but in time, the opportunity presents itself again. Also, take a certain strength from the idea that, in our perspective, the actions you do actually choose are rooted in the impetus to serve yourself. See if you can give up or look again at the idea that the mundane, the difficult things you seem mired in, are there as negatives to perhaps punish you or to be difficult for you. Look again at these times and think, 'Somehow the impetus of this was to serve.' Some part of you found a way to relate that served you when you were three, but it is not serving you at thirty-three. If you remember the impetus of action was somehow positive, it can allow a little change. It can release some rage. It can release some fear.

In the same way, if life continues in a certain way and your thinking focuses only on, 'I want this to be different. I want to be doing what I want to do,' stop and consider that there may be value in what is *actually* occurring. Rather than seeing that which is present as tripping you up or holding you back, take a moment and ask , 'Why are these things not aligned? How is my everyday life, just as it is, serving me?' As an example, it may be that the way of living which you experience as limited and negative, is really supportive and positive. A lifestyle may be giving you time and space to come into a further awareness of something. It could be that the ideal you hold in your head is not totally aligned or totally supportive of all your deeper needs in ways you do not consciously recognize.

If you can consider that life and your choices are somehow serving you, it may open up a whole awareness of how it *is* serving and why the action of your ideals has not yet occurred. We see that at times this is very frustrating, especially because there are shifts when you are really aligned to a new direction and the old direction is still occurring. This, though, is a reflection of your expansion abilities – your ability to perceive and sense something that is very far ahead in the time line. You may have an uncomfortable period when you are sensing that probability ahead of you, but your present reality is not there.

> The roots of actions are positive. Life is growth.
> We see life for people as having the same
> beautiful, blossoming naturalness as is reflected in nature.

You do not wonder why the plants chose to be planted in the rocky soil and still just naturally unfold. You, too, have made the choice of natural unfolding. You have the extra element of awareness of consciousness and co-creation. You have the choice to interact in your evolution with varying degrees of awareness and intensity.

71

We cannot stress enough that looking at life again – turning those parameters and constructs of thought around – can open new dimensions in your life, in you. Looking anew at life can even allow you to touch into other dimensions of reality. Even if those other dimensions never come into the consciousness, it is quite an exploration to look again at all of the variety one situation could hold if you simply turned it on its end.

When you permit conscious exploration of ideas, permission to experience another perspective is being created.

Once you begin to explore broader conceptualizations, you will find it difficult to easily go back into rigid parameters. Others might get a little impatient with you. They will say to you, 'Can't you just ever accept something the way it is? You're always looking at something another way!' This will start to happen and you will probably underestimate how challenging this can be to others. You may discover you are going to have to develop ways to explain your perspective through anecdote or example.

CHAPTER FIVE

WORKING WITH AWARENESS

Your inner sense is attuned to much more than you know;
to the moon, the sun, the earth - to everything.
It finds perfect times for you to do inner developmental work.

How do we deal with the fact of doubt about our information, and the information you bring to yourself? We don't 'deal' with it at all. Doubt exists. It is part of being human, part of this life. You can move the energy of doubt into discernment. We look at doubt and put it aside. Write it down in the margin, as it were. Then, go back and examine it. The inner sense is a wonderful judge. The only imperfectness about the inner sense is that sometimes its judgments are based on things that are far away from the conscious mind. Sometimes it isn't until much time has gone by that you can see why you made the decision you did. The inner sense is an accurate judge. Put the doubts where you can look at them again. The only difficulty with doubt is when you let it become a rigid hindrance, a wall to your own experience to discovering your own truth about whatever is sensed. You are the judge of your past, you are the creator of your progress, and the timing is always from your own inner sense of the appropriateness.

Your inner sense is attuned to much more than you know, finding perfect times and situations for your inner developmental work. As energy is mutable, your sense in the moment is the trustworthy source. Words of any guide or divining system or any element away from the present moment can most readily be contraindicated. The sense of the moment must be honored.

> The goal is to trust yourself.
> Your judgment is not untrustworthy.
> It is you who do not trust it.

When you find yourself judging, moving away, doubting the information, we suggest you take that healthy judgment (although we would modulate the word 'judgment' to *discernment*) and visualize this judgment within a locked box. Visualize the locked box put on the shelf for awhile. You do not have to get rid of the judgment. You do not have to immediately change this judgment. You simply have to allow yourself to put it aside. Let the information and awareness flow. You can reach discernment after you have received this information and permitted some level of integration. By placing doubt on the shelf, you can allow yourself to receive information and make considerations that rigid doubt may have forestalled.

> The Inner Awareness is attuned and
> pulsating in alignment with you.

How can you be sure the awareness you are receiving is accurate? The Inner Awareness is attuned and pulsating in alignment with you. Difficulty can come from the conscious mind's understanding or interpretation of the information received. We suggest you ask the question again and again, especially if it is a decision or idea outside of your everyday choices.

Check again. How to check? Ask yourself and listen. See if the answer comes again and again. This questioning leads to what we call visceral understanding. One hears people say, 'I just had a gut-level feeling,' and that is exactly what has occurred. Your inner being physically presents an answer, confirmation. When you feel a 'yes' within your physical body, it is a certain kind of knowledge that is almost touchable, almost able to be held in your hand. You all have experienced this. If you feel levels of ambivalence, we suggest you honor that unsettled sense, and do not take action on anything that is a 'No' on the visceral levels.

Eventually you will be able to tap into confirmation energy more and more consistently. When one takes an action from these inner answers, the choices can be extremely powerful because they reflect that all of you are in alignment. When you take actions based on these inner alignments, this aligned energy is recognizable to others. People will respond by saying, 'Although I don't agree with your choice, I can tell this is the one you are making.' They are acknowledging the power of aligned energy. Explore getting this sense of validity, for it builds within you the essential empirical history of accuracy for yourself. The more your whole being knows that you have given yourself correct information, correct awareness, the more you are then able to trust in yourself and to open and expand yourself to yourself.

RETROSPECT AS A TOOL

Retrospect is more than the fact that you
cannot see all of a process as it happens. It may be that there
are subtle processes not yet clear enough to be understood.

Remember, you are so much more than just your thoughts, your conscious mind. You have the ability to tap into all kinds of energy sources. Sometimes, translating that energy into conscious understanding does not happen or cannot happen because the energy itself is too mutable. This is why you must sometimes wait in the process called 'time' to get the understanding. Subtle processes that you can sense in some way often need linear time to become clear enough to be consciously comprehended in language and thought. Senses such as this are literally senses. There is not enough data, if you will, enough density of molecules to make form, even if it is in the form of a thought or a concept. Your brain cannot bring those subtle energy molecules and form them into a thought. Concrete thoughts are literally a density of an energy molecule. When you are sensing, you are literally sensing some kind of fluctuation, perhaps an influx. Time can allow these things to become dense, to become thoughts, realities, and form. Then you can understand them. It isn't magical. In our view, it is the way energy works.

It is important to allow the idea that those things you could not once understand can be looked at again in another manner.

When you look at your own life, you can see the tool of retrospect in action. You can all see how all those boring times, or painful times, or those times that really didn't seem to mean anything, did add up to something and had meaning you could not recognize at the time things were occurring. Allow yourself to look again at what you understand or feel you cannot yet understand. This does not mean you must doubt everything. It is only an element of *'Can you consider?'* Apply this especially to those things which you feel as negative. Remember, you may not always know how something works out until it has worked out. You may not consciously understand all that has occurred until retrospect brings you a broader perspective.

When you look back into your lives and see a terrible thing, and you see how, years later, you come to understand how the 'terrible thing' moved your life in a certain way, you demonstrate to yourself the tool of retrospect. Use this knowledge to sustain yourself through 'terrible things' with the consideration that there could be another element here. 'I can look at it another way.' Even if you cannot see the other way at that time, perhaps you can sustain yourself and give solace with the idea that conscious understanding is a bit down the road in time.

A willingness to accept that the direction or the outcome may change is a wonderful tool of balance.

When you are working with the inner sensing, goals and directions are tools. But a person who really is working in alignment might find that the direction set in February can be quite changed by July when a very different opportunity comes into their awareness for consideration. We want to encourage you to not be rigid. Although you set this direction in February, allow yourself to consider change. If you can allow fluidity, you might be able to perceive another entry into the scheme of things that might bring a twist and a turn and a choice that you literally had not imagined.

Willingness to accept new directions or other outcomes is so useful as a tool of balance. One may have an idea or sense of events and opportunities. You really feel that this is how you are going to direct your energy and you begin to follow that direction. As you are moving on this path you have set for yourself, you start to have a sense of, 'Oh, this project is moving in this other direction.' The sensitive person will say, 'All right, we'll see what's happening,' and allow themselves to move in the new direction. Another individual may choose, 'No, I want to do this and I am going to do this; this is how it must be,' continuing to direct the energy as they originally intended, according to their conscious program.

We encourage you to be willing
to be aware when the interactions of the Web
offer information that could change your direction.
Allow a willingness to consider this change.

It is useful and effective for individuals to place their energy in a direction. If you are looking for a job and are just waiting for the cosmos to give you the job, probably not much will occur. One sets a direction and begins looking for a job. The job may come as a direct result of your action, such as your responding to an ad in the newspaper. The job may come as well from an indirect reflection of your actions. You have focused your energy; you are definitely looking for a job; but, an old friend meets you on the subway, finds out your situation, and tells you of a job! In this situation you have an interconnection of allowing and permitting with conscious release of the outcome. You see, here you have set the direction, you are using your will and intent, but you are permitting the outcome to come from something other than the specific direction you initiated.

Life is all a flux.
You are never in only a receptive mode
or only a conscious mode.

The more you are aware, the more you permit yourself many levels of awareness; you can see life as movement. You readily accept that the physical body is doing many processes at once that you have no conscious idea of. Use this image to see these elements of awareness, of will, and direction happening in a

79

flowing and subtle manner. It is first grasping the idea that they are happening and then being willing to participate with them.

Explore the mundane.
Keep your theatre in the theatre. The subtle changes
you make will truly become integrated within you.

We encourage individuals to not need drama in their spiritual life. You do not have to be jumping out of your body, going through all of the past lives and fasting for three or four days and all of that sort of thing. You *can*, but you do not need to. Eventually it starts to interfere with our biggest theme, the 'long haul.'

Spiritual paths are expressions of what is already present within you and expressions of it in your everyday life, every day for all of it. As you can see, if your only way to touch into feeling centered or feeling Spirit or feeling nature, is always gut-wrenching dramatics, you are not going to live to be ninety-five or if you do, you are going to say, 'Well, I used to do that when I was younger, but I don't do it anymore.'

The more you do things for yourself in a
subtle way or towards subtlety,
the more growth is able to be sustained.

There is a great pull towards drama. But, you can have validity of change and progression without the pain and drama and difficulty. One does not need drama or trauma to grow. We would like to energize a slowing down of the spiritual pendulum. Spiritual aha's and peak experiences are often followed by deep feelings of separation and despair and doubt.

Drama and its accompanying intensity are often experienced as having more validity, more importance, and more truth. In theatre, the dramatic play is well respected. Comedy has its place, but does not receive the same respect. Many people interpret intensity and drama as real, as strength, as powerful. Culture and society often is not very interested in a lot of the subtleties. This same quest for drama is sought in some interpretations of spiritual teachings. People are allowing themselves to somewhat move away from restrained, painful limitations and discipline, but everyone still wants to have the feeling of being on the mountain top, popping out of the body and meeting spirits. It is a task to try to get people to accept the validity of more subtle interactions.

Your whole way of perceiving growth is centered around catharsis. What if you do not have a catharsis? If you hold the image of catharsis *only*, it will become the carrot before the donkey. It will pull you and drive you through class, through course, through seminar, through experience, through this, through that. What you might not be able to see is the ongoing subtleties, tones, shadings, and knitting - integration. Let yourself free from the idea that change only comes through expulsion, catharsis, release. Change can also come through grounding, through recognition, through acceptance.

DEFINING YOUR EXPERIENCE

You have the right to define your experience.

Remember, if you are having an intense experience, you are the creative element. You, therefore, have the power and the accountability within yourself to declare your needs in the experience. You can simply say, 'I do not want to participate in this.' Any time you have a connecting relationship, a connecting level, with more than yourself and it has become uncomfortable and not appealing to you, *disconnect*. State, 'I will not participate in this.' 'I am not participating in this.' Your ambivalence will keep the connection. Your declaration of your position will create the choice you want.

It does not serve for any of you to be buffeted by phenomena. You are all able to learn through subtlety. If you want intensity, you are able to have that in a way that is harmonious, balanced and serve you. If you find that in any way you are creating fear situations, take the time to look at why. Ask, 'Why am I trying to create this ambivalence?' 'Why do I want to separate from my path?' Be willing to be accountable for yourself.

It may not be your conscious thoughts. It may be the fear of the small child within. But, if you do not ask the question of the small child, you will not know that is what it is. Do not judge yourselves, either, as in, 'Oh, I'm being resistant.' Rather, examine and question. Always know you are co-creating. 'I will not.' 'I am not participating in this experience.' Close the door in the face of anything you do not want to participate in. You may also ask for the help of your guides, of your friends, whatever. Let anything energized as experiential occur in balance and harmony.

VALUING THE MUNDANE

Value the mundane aspects of your life.
Appreciate and value its constancy as a support to allow clarity.

When you have to make a choice, we always suggest you make the choice you feel most connected to. When choosing becomes simply overwhelming, return your focus to the mundane. Your everyday life is a thread that you notice seems to go on sometimes even without you. It is a movement. In times of stress what do people do? The everyday! They wash the dishes, they clean the floors. They do the laundry. They maintain their everyday life.

Many philosophies talk about living life as a meditation. Remember those words when you are overwhelmed, and return to, 'Well, I'm not going to think about that right now.' Very wise advice! When you go and do the laundry, there you are folding the clothes and all of a sudden you say, 'I'm not going to do that workshop.' Or you say, 'I'm worth the $150 cost and I'm going to do it.' Remember, the conscious mind has a narrower view. When you release the conscious perusal of the idea and focus on the mundane, you are allowing the Inner Awareness and Expanded Awareness to literally reach out and bring you information and alignment. Your energy links and lines up with the energy in the Web about you. The answer then can 'come' to you, 'pop' into your head. We see this as the natural way energy moves. Again, it is a variation of allowing and permitting.

Allow the glass to be empty so it may be filled.

There is always a need for balance when working with visualization or creating affirmations to bring something into your lives. Often it is advised one should use specifics and repetition to hold the energy. We see that too much intensity, in essence, creates such a vibration (you can picture it moving), that it works against receptivity. One must allow the glass to be empty, so it may be filled. If you are continually putting in energy, you cannot receive. If you are continually putting out energy, you cannot receive. Always balance your energy requests, your information requests, with times of what could be called passivity, but we would call *receptivity* – an allowing for the answer. You have put the letter in the mail. Now there is nothing more you can do – you have mailed it. So you must wait a period of time for the answer to come to you. Again, be comfortable with the flow of allowing and permitting.

DREAMS, IMAGES, ICONS

Immerse yourself in another kind of consciousness.

Do not forget about reading fiction as a tool of expansion. Reading science fiction, metaphysical fiction, magical fiction is a way to immerse yourself in another kind of consciousness. It gives the conscious mind another way to see things, even if that reality is not what will come. The more you can give new possibilities and alternative images to the conscious mind, the more your conscious mind is able to move into accepting the possibility of expanded realities for yourself.

All the associations that come to you in dreams have validity.

This does not mean that each association is, in and of itself, definite recall, and definite fact. But, it does mean that each association, each image, each scenario that comes to you is valid information. These images are icons of knowledge, symbols of belief, of yourself. They can be symbols of other elements of yourself, symbols of others you have been connected with. So suspend judgment. Suspend deciding, 'Well, this is just my imagination.' Of course, it might be your imagination, and is that not part of yourself bringing information?

We are asked, 'I tend not to remember my dreams. Is there a way I can be more aware of them?' If you desire, you can affirm that you have more memories. You can direct your experience. What might be more helpful is to affirm that you have the *information* from the dreams. This means you can allow the information to come forward as it will. It may not come upon waking, as you imagine it is to remember your dreams. Often people very much remember aspects of their dreams, but they do not attach the information to the dream state. We are asking you to expand your concept of what remembering your dreams is. You will soon find that many pieces of information that come into your awareness, sometimes abruptly, are indeed, garnered from your dream state.

Do not allow yourself to be dominated by your conscious ideals, images and desires.

Remember, these are *your* icons; your symbols of direction. When these images seem to be unfulfilled, stop a moment and say, 'What is that other sense of me creating, aside from what I can think about and conceptualize?' Icons are symbols one builds and also, symbols that can evolve. Icons can take conceptualizations that you have pondered over, conceptualizations that have just bubbled up and come to you – desires, wants, focuses – all realms of things, and make them clear for you.

Icons can become solid and this is when they interfere. Do not allow an icon to become rigid. Changing and modifying is an important element of icons. Using the idea of statuary, think instead of icons which can serve and do serve – not of plaster, not of stone, but of modeling clay. If you realize that an icon is of malleable clay and is not destroyed or ruined by addition or alteration, you can then view goals and directions that you form into symbols as mutable. Remember, you always have the right to re-form an icon. You can then use the icon as a tool to pull the energy, to send the energy, to hear and follow the energy. If you let your icon become as rigid as black marble or stone, the energy will not flow. A rigid icon will allow you to see and experience only one direction or possibility.

What we are really talking about is releasing the outcome. Set the direction. Let images form or form images specifically – allowing and creating icons. Know these are ways you are molding, modeling and integrating conscious and unconscious elements that are coming to you. But it is indeed only a model. It is a symbol of things known and unknown. It is a goal you make use of, but allow a willingness to have the goal change, to have the icon become as it will, which may be different than your original intent.

Hold these ideas in the back of the mind, as a principle. When you find yourself getting into a situation that doesn't seem to move and isn't turning out how you want it to be, no matter what you seem to do, is this the time for a thought about your icon? Is it clay or is it stone? Let yourself re-examine. If you are hitting a stone wall, don't think, 'What am I doing wrong?' Instead, ask, 'What else can I be seeing here?' Because if it is not happening as you imaged it, it may not be that you are doing things wrong. It may be that you are not paying attention to what you, in most probability, are doing right! Often when you re-think it, you laugh, because it becomes clear.

> Allow an image, a symbol of
> the perfection of yourself
> to come to your awareness.

This is not a process of thinking; it is one of *allowing* a tool in the form of a symbol to come to you. When you need energy, when you need balance, when you need strength – this symbol will be a link you can call upon. A link you can feel within you. A link that connects you with guides, with comfort, with support – by

87

allowing you to connect with the perfection of yourself and through that perfection allowing you to experience a connection, which you are quite capable of having, with All There Is. The symbol can be visual, can be musical, can be words, can be a texture. It can be whatever in whatever form. Later it can be appropriate to attach the symbol to a concrete form, if you desire. You may fuse it in a crystal. You may draw it. You may carve it in wood.

> **It is a true gift for you to experience a tiny bit of how you are seen and felt by others.**

Those symbols of stars and water and snowflakes and birds and all that may come to your awareness are loving icons of the energy of yourself. It is a *reflection* of what qualities of you are recognized and experienced by others. It is a true gift for you to experience a tiny bit of how you are seen and felt by others. You are giving and sharing people. Every day you affect and touch and are meaningful to people you don't know, as well as to those you do, because you bear with you energy that is clear, loving and beautiful.

EXPLORATION & GROWTH

In your searching, in the quests you set for yourself, your greatest contribution is that you share the energy of 'I seek to understand'. It pulsates about you, even when you do not share it verbally. People experience you as understanding because of this.

**Your conscious willingness to explore,
allows other people to explore.**

When search and exploration becomes a dominant factor in your life, know that this quest is the way you serve and connect. The outward things you put your energy into are reflections of that. Your whole being, especially through conscious willingness to explore, allows other people to explore. Many of you have had lessons and explorations allowing people to be as they are, which sometimes means you have to release them or release from them in your daily interactions. Allowing others this freedom to be as they are is a gift you give. Giving it has made each of you who have explored this stronger in ways you do not even know. Your symbol also holds all these vibrations and will act for you as a link to experiencing qualities of yourselves. Your icon will assist you to experience the centeredness that is available to people who can acknowledge and allow connection with All There Is.

**You can gather balance and strength from the
direct connection you all have to Source energy.**

When you are overwhelmed and stymied by the vast difficulties and paradoxes of society, we suggest you anchor within yourself and into your life and your vibrations. You must tune in and reconnect with your spiritual essence. It is not that you are specifically connecting to a great guide that will speak to you and direct you. It is more that you are connecting to the pulsation of existence we are all part of. That pulsation will strengthen you, like the infant baby listening to the heartbeat of the mother. In most situations, one cannot completely cope with the whole of a situation at once, as it is of too much complexity. You can take some action, some direction, from your own inner being.

The concept of growth and movement is reflected in all images of spirituality.

Spiritual expression and connecting through the Inner Awareness is not something that is achieved. It is not 'gotten.' It is a process developed consistently and constantly. One touches in again and again. Balance is not achieved – rather, balance is found in the movement of balanc*ing*. You will never get there. Even when you are gone from this form, you do not get there. Life continues. Life is motion. The concept of growth and movement is reflected in all images of spirituality – spirals, helixes, mandalas, lotuses, etc. Feeling out of balance is natural. One then re-balances. People seek the ability to rebalance quickly and with more and more consistency. People seek to learn to touch into the inner self and experience connectedness. Again, this is why we caution people against always seeking catharsis or great spiritual 'highs'. Seeking catharsis creates a spirituality, a spiritual expression, only of these intense moments. Allow yourself to discover your own ways of balance and connection. Find your own way to discover, experience and move with the ebb and flow of energy as it occurs in your life, not as you think it should be.

CHAPTER SIX

RELATING WITH AWARENESS

*We encourage you to honor doubt, fear,
and ambivalence as valid information.*

Ambivalence should be respected. When you are not sure of something, it might be other than the psychological term, 'resistance.' It might, indeed, be accurate information. It may be your inner awareness saying, 'We're not sure about this. We don't have all the information we need.' We very much encourage you to honor your doubts, fears, and ambivalence as valid information. Dislike and negativity may also be communicating a truth that needs to be considered. Rather than accepting the idea that you have a negative core which you must keep trying to make right, consider the idea that under any negative core is perfection. One needs to permit this perfection to blossom. Embrace also that there is wisdom within you, not only fear. In fact, your interpretation that it is only fear without substance or accuracy may be what is actually inaccurate.

The reality of that which is interpreted by the conscious mind as fearful, disturbing or bothering (particularly in the sleep state), is often different than the terms describe. Strong emotions or new awareness can be interpreted by the conscious mind as negative, fearful or disruptive. Yet, is it truly disruptive or is it, instead, overwhelming? Allow yourself to look at things from another view.

When you feel a fear is beginning to limit you, see if you can find other ways to comfort and support yourself. Comfort and support is what you seek when you are controlled, directed or stopped by fear. Often, it is more an ambivalence than truly wanting to stop or not go forward. You want to feel support; a strong foundation within yourself.

Allow yourself to explore how, in some way, relationships have served, fulfilled or added to some aspect of yourself. When a pattern occurs again and again, and you become frustrated with your seeming inability to change the pattern, it may be that some part, some aspect of the psyche is connected with the energy from that pattern, even while 95% of you have evolved away from the pattern.

PATTERNS GROW FROM POSITIVE IMPETUS

**When an action is created over and over again in a life,
it is not necessarily from a negative source.**

Here, as we said earlier, an aspect of you feels at the root of the pattern, at its impetus, a positive connection to the action. The difficulty lies in that much of the rest of you has matured to a different position. The question is asked, 'It seems I have had a pattern of recurring involvements with people who are not especially nurturing or healthy for me, and yet I am extremely nurturing for them...I'd like to know what I can do to break the pattern.'

Knowledge of a positive impetus can serve in
allowing and permitting change through
diffusing elements of fear and guilt.

We suggest you let the inner self reveal to you how you have benefited from these relationships. You might choose to sit and work with a journal. Ask yourself questions and write down the answers that come to you most immediately. Perhaps when you see what positive element has been given to you, you will be able to understand how you might be able to satisfy that aspect in another way, meet that need in another way. Our questioner can ask, 'How am I fulfilled by nurturing others? How can I experience this fulfillment in a more balanced way?'

In the same vein as fear, self-limitations can be seen as a comfort device. Consider again the principle that individuals do not choose actions for negative reasons. Consider that some component within the individual always chooses an action which would be the most beneficial. Unfortunately, as we have all observed, very often the actions are not beneficial to the total aspect of the person in the present context, since the sense of benefit originated at another time. Knowledge of the positive impetus of patterns can allow change through understanding and comprehension.

ON RELATIONSHIP

A relationship is a coming together of energies. And the relationship, in and of itself, becomes a living being.

A relationship evolves from two energies merging in a way that is different than two singular ones. Coming into this merged state, the relationship follows its own paths and patterns; its own pulls and awareness. Strife typically comes into a relationship when the two participants have very specific ideas and expectations of how the relationship must be and are uncomfortable or unwilling to let the relationship evolve according to its own natural path.

Looking again at ideas and expectations might open the energy of the relationship. We suggest you begin a dialogue. One tool is to write down a question, as in, 'What do I believe or mean by *relationship*?' Talk with that part of you that is holding certain expectations and parameters about what and how you and your partner should be relating to each other. You might be surprised to discover how specific your inner senses, or some part of your inner beliefs, are dictating how things should be. It might give you an ability to let go or reprocess some of those things and let the relationship grow more naturally.

Go into separate rooms and really see what your inner selves say. Write down 'How I feel supported by you.' 'How I want you to support me.' 'How I want you to act.' 'How should people act when they are angry?' 'How should we feel about fidelity?' Look again at what your lives actually create. People often believe that their ideals are how the reality should be and do not question those base assumptions. The reality you expressed unconsciously and consistently also has validity and truth.

**The reality of your life *as it is*
needs to be looked at and learned from.**

Whatever you think you *should* be doing, you *are* doing what is occurring now. You cannot bring what you do into alignment with an ideal, until you first acknowledge what it is you are doing now. What need is being met there? What needs are being served by living your life as you have been? Look at things again. Look again at what has been distressing or disturbing to you. Turn them around 180 degrees and see how they would look from the whole other side. This time of exploring these inner thoughts is not a time to take action. Explore through looking, questioning, examining. Use the information gained to open up your attitudes and to reconnect with a better understanding of your own perspective. Action, choices, decisions can be made when information is more fully known and understood.

**Parameters and structure, when used
in balance, can serve a situation.**

Difficulties in relationships demonstrate and reflect the fluctuations of life and relationships. We speak of the long haul on the spiritual path. The culture and individuals often do not hold the long view or the historical view, and this is so in relationships as well. In other times and places, where commitment offered few options, people knew a relationship was for the long haul. A positive by-product of this approach was that they were more accepting of the ebbs and flows, the fluctuations and disconnections that naturally occur in a long process. We do not suggest people relinquish the options available in today's society, nor judge them; rather, we ask you to explore ideas of time and commitment. We remind you that an essential element of relating is a construct of time to grow in.

When you have a five-week class, you can think, 'If I didn't get to say it on day one, I still have some more time.' If you thought the class might end at a moment's notice, you might grow uncomfortable, worrying, 'If the class ends today, I might not get to ask my question or learn what I wanted to learn.' When you allow yourself to make a statement of commitment, it might be easier in those times when energy is unaligned or not flowing to simply move through it. You can then say, 'Well, we went through that and we thought it was the end of the world. But, guess what? Its just part of being in relationship.' Some stresses come from expectations, often unspoken or unrecognized. In current culture we see a pressure towards quick 'perfection' within a relationship, with people quickly deciding it is time to exit and begin their search for this perfection once again.

Making an agreement of commitment acts as a support and foundation.

Setting up an acknowledged structure of commitment, a statement of commitment, gives you a certain freedom to know, 'It might be weird right now, but at least we still have some time until we have to make a decision.' Otherwise, everything is of the moment. Often the view is, 'If this is wrong now, it's all over.' People do not allow themselves any leeway. Making an agreement of commitment, be it for six months, a year or indefinitely, acts as a support and foundation. Such agreements are an example of how parameters and structure, created with balance and agreement, can serve a situation. Remember these structures can be mutable, re-evaluated and recreated. View structure as a support, not a confinement.

We encourage each of you to let yourselves explore the plethora of loving relationships available.

Culture can be limited in how it permits individuals to be intensely involved with each other. The lover or marriage image is the predominant ideal. Friends and others, who share intensities similar to the couple arrangement, are often looked upon askance or expected to give up such intensities when one bonds with a partner.

Allow yourself to explore the many aspects of love and caring relationships which can be available to you. In allowing this expansion in personal ways, you are also laying the groundwork for expansion, contact and understanding of other communities and cultures, as well as truly other realities. Exploring new realities in your personal realm supports the concept of other realities and the concept of expanding the nature of all realities.

Some expressions of love never need physical or even verbal expression. There is a creative power in the energy of loving. Acknowledge it. Accept and receive it. What you then experience is a real bonding and sense of communion. Many of you have had or have such friends. Culture still maintains a separation between friends, supporters and the primary relationship. We encourage you to allow an expanded and integrated view of relating.

Jealousy is not to be judged.
It can be used as a tool of awareness.

Here again, we must consider paradox. Jealousy exists. It is usually an expression of fear, of self-fear and inadequacy. There indeed may be reality to the situation. When one has set up the parameters of a relationship, if another person breaks that parameter, then the relationship is threatened. People must consciously come into alignment about the precepts and principles they share with each other. Jealousy occurs and grows if dialoguing is not done. Two individuals can be romantically loving and really never have an idea of 'Do you think fidelity is the ultimate requirement or do you not?'

Dialoguing with the self can serve, again, to reveal hidden expectations and misunderstandings. Jealousy is not to be judged; it is a tool. It is a clue that something is out of alignment. Even if one person is irrationally jealous, that quality then becomes something in and of itself for the other person to examine. 'Can I give enough to make a person who is so frightened feel safe? Do I want to give so much to make this person feel safe?' Use the red flag of jealousy as a tool of understanding. If not addressed and explored, jealousy will undermine any relationship, be it between friends, lovers or colleagues.

> ### Sometimes anger is exactly the balance point to change the situation.

Harmony and balance seem like unquestioned ideals and beneficial, but at times a true gut response – 'Go away. Don't ever come here again.' – is the fullest, most truthful and appropriate response. Clearly state how the situation is and the person can clearly feel it. Anger can be fully appropriate. Even rage. It can be the balance point. How many of you have thrown things around, screamed and yelled, and then come into a real centering and awareness of yourself? Don't fall into the idea that the spiritual person never yells. This is a limiting, one-way image. Allow yourself, in your spirituality, to explore all the elements of living. Remember, balancing and harmony are active states and can be experienced in many modes.

FORGIVENESS & ACCEPTANCE

The ideal of forgiveness is a good one.
But more practical is the ideal or tool
of observation, consideration,
acknowledgment and acceptance.

The past always has elements of discovery and understanding. When one allows rigidity and closure of parameters about the past, when one carries these as guilt, such elements can literally become encapsulated in energy and create an actual knot of energy. People often refer to the idea of an emotional wound or tenderness, as in, 'I feel hurt from that time. It is still a tender spot. It's a button.' These phrases are accurate descriptions of the results of an actual energy process.

The idea of forgiveness draws us, but often this ideal is difficult to fully implement. Often people want to forgive, but instead leap over their feelings to a false mental state of the *idea* of forgiveness. What is often more accessible is the ideal or tool of observation and consideration; acknowledgment and acceptance. Observe. Consider all the elements; consider that there may be elements unknown. Acknowledge your own actions, acknowledge the action of another. Accept the actuality of the moment. Accept the paradoxical, and at times conflicting, nature of emotions and understanding. Acceptance permits integration of the tender energy spots, allowing them to reunite with the whole of your being and in that, become less tender. Through acceptance and allowing integration, you will find that you can easily and naturally discover the energy and release of true forgiveness.

If it is a pattern of your own that concerns you – 'Why have I done this? Why does this occur?' – look at an action or pattern and say, 'How did this in some way serve me? What part of me felt this would serve?' In this way, you might discover some pattern of behavior which served you very well when you were five, a withdrawal perhaps, which does not serve you as well when you are thirty-nine. If you discover there was an element that made sense to that five-year-old child in you, this will aid you in coming into an acceptance of your choices and actions.

> Acceptance levels lead to integration
> levels which will lead to release.
> Release of fear and guilt.

Rather than casting out, getting rid of, or releasing the patterns, you need to *embrace* the pattern, making it part of the whole. An element within you that is out-of-synch with the whole will always catch you. As you worked through observation to acknowledgment and acceptance, dissonant elements of you become a part of the whole and integrated. You suddenly realize the issue has softened. It is no longer a tender spot. Look at the past with a different viewpoint. Do not replay again and again the same old story you hold in your memory, but truly look at it anew. Ask, 'All right. What good was going on here?' and see what you can come up with. You might find it a very interesting exploration, with a new and different perspective awaiting you.

However you image the Source,
know that the inner self of you
is of that same perfection.

Consider the idea of surrendering to self-acknowledgment, self-acceptance, self-forgiveness, and self-love. And through this process, surrendering to the perfection within you that is a holographic element of the Source energy of us all. The idea of surrender seems to make many uncomfortable. 'Surrender' here is not a quality of being overpowered and giving up under duress. Rather, surrender is an allowing and permitting, an unfolding, in complete trust and deep inner knowing, to the energy of creation which is expressed in your dear and precious essence of being.

Perfection and the perfection of all creation exist.
It is present.
It does not need to be created by you.

For one to surrender the fullness of their true being, one usually must begin with forgiveness. So many of us do not recognize the perfection inherent in each being. We do not see ourselves as that sustaining energy, as that loving energy, that in most cases we seek from without. We wish to remind you, to energize within you, the idea again of the image coming to your conscious mind of your perfection. Your perfection and the perfection of all creation exist. It is present. It does not need to be created by you. It does not need to be gotten and received. Perfection is present. Its pulsation is steady, constant, consistent, at all times available. And the further pulsations, the connecting links, are present in the same way at all times.

Opening up to oneself is a literal process.

It is a process initiated by your cooperative energy systems, by your intent, by your desire. Yet, it is also a natural process, which means that although you can set out the intent clearly, definitely, with specifics, it is not something you can force. It is allowing. It is permitting. Bringing the concept of this process to your conscious mind is one of the beginning steps.

THE PERFECTION WITHIN

If you cannot accept the wisdom and perfection within yourself, you can imagine the possibility.

Surrender. Know that the inner self of you is of the same perfection as however you image the Source. We encourage each of you to reaffirm your wisdom, to reaffirm to yourself your own perfection. If you cannot accept the wisdom and perfection within yourself, you can imagine the possibility. If you cannot see it for yourself, perhaps you can see it for another, a child, a loved one, and in that, discover it is available for you as well. Allow yourself to experiment with feeling into this concept, even if it is at moments uncomfortable. Give your conscious mind ways to explore this concept. Feel a tenderness towards yourself as you would to a growing child. Feel a forgiveness as you would to one who has survived a great difficulty. Feel a love for yourself. Allow one moment of that love which you are so willing to give to others to be mirrored to yourself.

CHAPTER SEVEN

AWARE LIVING

Allow the evolution of your own belief system.

It is our desire to assist in your ability to create and follow your own philosophical, spiritual and emotional belief system – through the integration of information from outward sources and personal growth experiences with the inner core knowledge each of you possesses. In our view, there is no caution or worry that there would be total unrelated diversity without any cohesion of beliefs.

Inner core principles are extant and exist as available energy for all humankind. We hold that there is a positive pulsation principle inherent in each human being; to us, this positive pulsation is inherent in all life forms. Thus, the idea that at some timing all living beings and energies can have a common unity is not farfetched. Therefore, it is easy for us to accept that, as we set up the energy of empowerment, there is safety in that each of you will reveal to yourself the same principles - altered to fit your understanding – but the core will not be altered.

We need not describe or give or reveal one by one these principles. This is the task of your personal evolution. What you will find experientially is – as this information integrates, as awareness flows within and without, as the principles become known in your life – you will know the serenity and security of coming into Truth. Society and culture continues to hold ideas of authority and a singular way. The idea that the individual has valid core knowledge and awareness within is still a new concept.

**Consider redefining your ideas and concepts
of belief and being a believer.**

It is essential that you permit yourself to hold your personal synthesis and understanding of the nature of being, of the nature of reality, of the nature of other realities. Allow the self to become aware of, to discover and build upon your sense of integrity and belief; including, perhaps, belief in things mystical, mysterious, magical. This is a challenge for many of you in your society. Many of you permit yourselves intellectually to explore phenomena, as long as you maintain a certain distance. Indeed, as long as you do not step into the realm of belief – belief as considering and perhaps, accepting, the validity of the essence of your direct experience.

Believing does not mean one simply casts aside conscious thought, intellectual pursuit, and totally accepts philosophies. It need not mean you enter into specific practices that are given to you without consideration, or that you must unquestioningly follow certain social, dietary and emotional rules. Instead, give yourself permission to feel on the inner levels, knowledge and information, sensings about your reality. Again and again we use phrases such as 'letting it come to you,' 'I feel that' or 'I know that.' Such approaches of allowing are tools to develop and expand your awareness. These are positive tools which will not make you less; and especially will not make you less of a thinking, conceiving, practical individual. Rather, using them will permit you to expand and integrate all aspects of your awareness.

What a challenge it is to take a concept you hold dear, one you have lived by for many years and allow yourself the privilege of turning it around 180 degrees and looking at it again in a totally different light. We encourage all of you to allow yourselves to be comfortable, to believe in your ability to have wisdom and to accurately discern information. Permit yourself to look at and perhaps, sometimes take action toward things, ideas and choices, in a way you have not before.

You draw your system of beliefs to you.

We remind each of you that you drew the system of beliefs to you. If it is necessary - in some greater whole, in the greater scheme, for your belief system to change unto itself, change away from itself, or for you as the individual to leave a system - it is a strength and support to remember you were expressing your spiritual essence present within you through that system. Although the system served to facilitate and direct you, it was your inner self choosing the alignment of expression.

There is no ordained, singular way for human beings to express themselves in the world.

We see no unchanging, ordained, mandated, singular, right or correctness to life. You can see *aspects* of validity in most every kind of expression. This, of course, does not mean you must embrace or take upon yourself ways of being you are not aligned to. It does not mean you must condone or support ways of being that you find painful or offensive or, in your view, morally wrong. When one feels lack of support for some structure, it is in alignment for a person to speak out and direct energy into making a change. Yet, you will find that when you release the mind from holding absolutes, the freer energy flow can lead you to understanding and perspectives that become unavailable through a narrow or rigid perspective.

Hold the idea of discernment, not judgment.

We would like to remind you that being able to consider an aspect of value in the most extreme position, does not directly lead to the conclusion that there should then be no discernment, or that you should participate in actions that are in an extreme position. Rather, we are encouraging you to acknowledge another perspective. Consider, at least intellectually, the idea that there could be validity in some aspect of the other person's actions or positions. This establishes an important point of tolerance. We encourage you to simply reserve a small part of the observation that truths of one time or place are, at times, not the truths of another time or place.

There is a wonderful fluidity inherent in being human.

It is disconcerting to some that we see no over-all, all-inclusive spiritual rules and regulations. No extant morality guidebook. However, this does not mean you should not participate in any measure in the moral codes of your reality. It is a gentle reminder that these codes evolve for purpose, through need, to serve a time and place. They are valid and essential, but not directives from a higher authority. You can look at your own historical times and see how what is acceptable and not acceptable changes and fluctuates. It reminds you of the wonderful fluidity that is inherent in being human, in being a being on this planet. Before you find yourself moving into judgment on yourself or others, perhaps you can take a moment to consider this idea.

A technique to bring balance, to regain centeredness,
is to bring your energy and focus to the present moment.

When individuals become overwhelmed by the broadness of their philosophical perspective – such as when one tries to contemplate the universe or the immensity of all time and such vast concepts – it is very easy to then find yourself out of balance. When the broad perspective overwhelms you, bring your energy, bring your focus – the emotional focus, the intellectual focus, the knowledge-based focus – to the present moment. In the situation of the 'moral code,' we remind each of you that you are present in this timing, in this society. However alienated you might feel, however separated you at times might feel, you are part and parcel of this greater whole.

We remind you to touch into yourself, to the values you have experienced, the values you hold true, the values you wish to participate with – and know that there is a correctness, that there can be an alignment – even if your ability to conceive of perspectives very vast may show you these values you hold are not a totality. It is still a correct choice, an appropriate choice, to interact with the values you hold.

Holding a broad spiritual perspective,
rather than taking away a value system,
gives you more responsibility towards accountability
to be aware of and to honor the values you hold.

Honor your own wisdom. Keeping the broad perspective can balance that your judgment and discernment does not move into a narrow vision, does not move into bigotry and prejudice. Do not use the idea of broad perspective to take away your ability to root into or to comfortably participate with your own value system, personal and societal. This participation is important. You are doing things of balance and value when you discover and link with values you hold dear and interact with.

The spiritual perspective asks of you to be willing to consider another's perspective. It asks you to consider the whole of a situation, how your own wants and needs interact with and affect another's and the world you all share. Having a broad spiritual perspective asks you to have integrity within yourself to the energy you are aligned to. It asks, also, a certain optimism; and that you can hold the balance of knowing your personal actions may not, in and of themselves, change a complete whole, but rather, may add an element, a note of change or sustenance.

So for those of you who begin to feel overwhelmed or begin to feel your actions and beliefs do not matter in the long run, we emphasize that it does indeed matter in the long run. The idea that there is balance and harmony in all things does not mean that everything and anything is 'okay.' It does mean that as life evolves, different choices, different actions can be experienced, can come into different balances and different effects, and in the long, long run there can be a balancing. Yet, on the personal, one-to-one, individual basis, it is essential for each individual to act with one's own integrity level and awareness, with ones own accountability and responsibility.

INDIVIDUAL IN SOCIETY

How else you can look at the fear of being different?
Can you consider asking,
'How does how I *am* serve myself, society and the world?'

Many spiritual pioneers fear being different and feeling disconnected from society. There are many elements in society where a person might feel outside. Perhaps you are of a different color. Perhaps you are of a different sexual orientation. Perhaps you are even of the wrong gender, such a basic thing as that. But, for many of you, there is often simply the sense, perhaps on a spiritual level, that you are somehow disconnected. There is no individual human being that is totally, in all aspects, congruent

110

with society. Any society is a unit of varying particles, making agreements and maintaining the agreements that are made. Individuals are required to find balance by modifying their energy to create the larger form, society. Even the person who seems to be following every idea and treatise of society, truly on some level, in some aspect, at times has to modulate action or beliefs to continue to fit into the idea of society.

Think of society as a unit made up of these varied and many particles. Uniqueness moves toward the general, becoming the average or typical, which creates a spaciousness to contain the many variations. It is a natural aspect of humankind to follow this movement from the individual into the society, inherently carrying an energy of balance. When you can consider it in this way, you may feel less constrained by the moments of modulation you experience.

The ideals of your society should, in some aspect, empower you to be the individual.

Let us acknowledge there is great power in the society. In particular your society, which not only was brought together through many people consciously choosing agreement, but principles of this society were brought through inner awareness processes. It is one of the few societies that created its principles of being through these processes. These very self-same principles should empower you. The idea, the ideals of your society should in some aspect empower you to be the individual. It is not simply chance that you have all chosen to live in this timing, in this place.

When you are feeling alienated, use your historical information, let your inner knowledge and your conscious knowledge support your idea that you can be very much who and what you are where you are. Be gentle with yourselves and acknowledge that it can be difficult to be an individual not fully in line with society.

Fear can come from holding rigid expectations and closed views, narrowing the parameters of how you experience life. For those of you that find you already, in the greater scheme of things, have made a choice that set you outside of the society you presently live in, can you consider looking at that as a positive? Yes, you are aware of the negative aspects, but can you just look again and look at the positive aspects by thinking, 'This somehow serves me and serves society and the world.'

The more you create the energy of
centeredness and acceptance within you,
the less difficulty you will have with how individuals,
and society in general, respond to you.

Many people who follow what is called the spiritual path, find themselves also outside of the mainstream. Rather than holding the image of yourselves as an alternative society, see yourselves, in a less judgmental way, as another aspect of society. You are choosing to explore another aspect of the whole. The more secure, centered, and accepting you are of yourself, of your position, your being and nature – the more you create that energy of centeredness and acceptance within you – the less difficulty you will have with how others respond to you. Intellectually people may not accept your position, but if you as an individual are anchored in the energy of your own acceptance, they will respond to that acceptance energy. They will tangibly feel the power of your inner security. Perhaps they will say, 'Well, I don't like your kind of people, but you are all right.' Of course, being the exception is not enough, but it is a beginning. One individual holds the energy of change that becomes the foundation of further change.

Each individual act is always of value.

Never underestimate the effect of the one individual, for that is really all you can focus upon. You can work toward greater situations. You can support greater situations. But, it is always your energy as the individual that is your essential focus and your contribution. Each individual act is always of value, as each of you are always of value.

View change as a natural expression of life.
Be willing to explore accepting change.

Change and growth cycles of living are often experienced as distressing and disruptive. A root essence of discomfort is often based on a person's inability to understand why change is occurring, for what purpose. We ask you to consider that meaningful occurrences are interwoven into the fabric of life and that one does not always recognize them as they occur. Value that the mundane is anchored in meaning and is of importance. Your life, your everyday life, is of importance. It is indeed your focus of exploration and meaning. Through daily living you are expressing energies, you are discovering. Each day you are exploring elements of the self that you may have no conscious awareness of. Time and the tool of retrospect will eventually bring further understandings. Look into nature to be reminded how change is the natural expression of life. See how things disintegrate, come apart and then re-grow. Release the idea of change as negative and destructive. Choose to anchor to the alignment you are feeling and be willing to accept, or explore accepting, the change.

BALANCE & BALANCING

**It is a perfectly natural state to be off-balance.
It is just as natural to rebalance and find alignment.**

It is not necessary for you to continually be swept about by your emotions and fears, as you move through change. During times of change it is appropriate to allow yourself to experience feeling overwhelmed and depressed and exhausted for a time. But, when the time continues on, it is your right to declare to yourself that you do not wish to continue with this draining experience of fear and emotion. If you cannot make this statement with full conviction, begin to do it with small steps. When you are out of balance, take a moment to calm yourself. Stop moving. Be still. Perhaps literally embrace and hold yourself. State, 'I am now feeling alignment. I am now feeling centeredness. I am going to sit still and get calm.' Do for yourself what you would do for a small child that was overwhelmed. Hold a stuffed animal! Do something to link in to what you would have done as a child, as someone who has not yet any tools for re-balancing.

Balance is not a static state. It is balanc*ing*.

Give yourself permission to find ways to move from the off-balanced state. You will find that any effort you make for yourself, no matter how small – simply making yourself a cup of tea and sitting down and making yourself drink it slowly – will begin to allow you to allow yourself to come to calmness, to centeredness.

Balancing is of paramount importance in true communication.

As individuals come into alignment with their beliefs and understanding of the world, they may be drawn to communicate their ideals through work that exemplifies these beliefs. Balancing is of paramount importance in true communication. Consider the intensity and sincerity of this questioner: 'I work for a group... trying to help our plane ... through the cooperative use of space technology, where we view earth as a complete spaceship or biosphere in which all nations' problems are interconnected and related, and that solutions require global applications of space technology that humans have created. In the course of my work I can talk to people and they intuitively understand what we are trying to accomplish; just mentioning this turns the switch and we work together. Other people don't understand at all or I meet people at all different stages of understanding what we are trying to accomplish. My question is why is that so and also is there something I can do that can help other people understand this process faster, so that these things can be implemented quicker and help the planet more efficiently?'

There is always a dilemma when one's view, which is totally aligned to the individual, and seems to be an aligned proposition in general, is not aligned to each and every person. One of the paradoxes of life is that seemingly reasonable understandings of the nature of reality are rejected by many other people. We remind you, paradox is the natural way of this world. You will find that the more you are willing to let go of rigid expectations of the outcome – to not demand a connection with every person, to not hold such a definite view of the total correctness of your view – in essence, the more you are willing to value each connection and accept non-connection, the more you will feel success and communication.

Again, if you are unable to alter the whole of the fabric of the politics or the society, it does not mean that, in a larger view, you have been unsuccessful or done nothing. You are the note in the symphony. It is often the case that a person follows the inner awareness and impulses without having the outward support of 'I completely changed this.' 'Completely' is the word that frustrates. Rather, focus on the specific. 'I changed Miss Jones' view.' 'I shared with Mr. Smith.' In the specific there is complete success. One can hold too strongly to the views of what has not been done. This is the idea of 'Is the glass half full or is it half empty?' Yes, it is frustrating when one holds such a strong principle and is not able to communicate it.

Although you may find support in the idea that there is
an ultimate cosmic balancing of all things, in the
everyday world you must cope with and accept paradox.

In the greater, fuller sense, living is not simply a rigid cosmic morality of rights and wrongs. In the furthest degree, balancing of all of the seeming paradoxes can occur. The problem is, although this ultimate balancing is a philosophical aspect that can support you, life requires you to cope with and accept paradox. You must take the actions you feel are necessary and correct. You must follow what you are aligned to, even if your actions do not seem to directly create change.

Communicating through the personal allows real feelings to be
shared and facilitates linking and connecting with another.

A successful communication technique is to share from the personal. 'I feel this is a legislation, a petition, a lobbying that really would have a positive effect... I feel that this element must be corrected or seen in another light...' When one presents a view *at* someone, sharing as if this is the only perspective, people are not given a way to open and respond with you. Some individuals will begin closure towards you, even if they agree with the view. When you share *of* yourself, you essentially invite them to hear your view. You literally open the energy system of exchange, so they may share with you. Responses may come as, 'Yes, I've often thought that.' They may say, 'Well, I'm not sure about all this, but I'm going to think about it.' The key is you have then allowed and invited their response.

Again, clear communication is facilitated through personal sharing. In the personal realm, intensity is fully appropriate. People are very able to respond to 'This man feels this so strongly.' But when you force a philosophy upon them, they hear, 'This man thinks I must think as he does.' You are not permitting them to agree with you. You are telling them they are less if they do not. Even if this is not your conscious intent, the force of the energy could easily be interpreted as such.

People have difficulty with aspects of themselves that do not fit into their personal belief system of how they should be.

A questioner shares feelings that touch many in the group. 'I am familiar with a slow and steady progression in my ongoing awareness and am troubled particularly with the moments when the glamour or the thrill or the ecstasy of another discovery or an integrated discovery, has worn smooth and is not part of my life and I am looking for the next step. And I find in that pause that parts of me unhealed, parts of me unschooled, come back to the surface to play themselves out. I'm thinking in terms of immoral thoughts, almost impish thoughts that another part of me is afraid will interfere with my progress, so-called, and I'm curious of a way to incorporate those moments and appreciate them, because they must have tremendous value to be there.'

We suggest a reconsideration of what is shared here. Some of the difficulty in this position is the narrowing of perceptions in the personal belief system. Here the words 'steady progression' are used, instead of words such as blossoming, allowing, exploring, or evolving. Even in science, the idea of evolution is not seen as a steady progression, but one with shifts and movements. The phrase 'steady progression' creates a limited view of how one must grow. The other phrases inherently hold images of fluidity.

People have difficulty with the aspects of their being that do not fit into how you feel, perceive, and image, the spiritual man that you are, should be, must be, will be. It is not that you have failed in your spirituality; it is that you are not allowing the construct or *image* of what the spiritual man is, to grow. Thus the inner self, those aspects of yourself you are consciously uncomfortable with, wish to live. Those aspects wish to be expressed, to blossom and it seems that they disconcertingly do just that. Look at the images you hold and see if you can soften the rigid outlines of expectation. See if you can try to recognize that you are working with an image. You need not replace the image, but rather let it evolve. Let your being show you what there is to see about yourself, instead of you trying to push or pull yourself into an image.

Humans have the great gift of allowing innate knowledge to work in combination with conscious intent, will and intelligence.

Allow yourself to be comfortable with yourself. Trust that if you are comfortable, if growth is perhaps easy, it is still of value. People become very invested in the idea of growth only through stretching, sacrifice, overcoming, routing out ideas. Do not bind yourself with a singular image. The flower pushes up from the earth by a steady

119

pulsation and then allows a blossoming from the innate essence of its being. Humans have the great gift of allowing innate knowledge to work in combination with conscious intent, will and intelligence. Yet such growth is still natural and can, at times, occur with ease. Ease can be valued as much as pushing.

CAREER & SPIRITUALITY

**The two elements of work –
the inner work and money-creating abilities –
can be separate, yet aligned and working side by side.**

Many people follow the philosophy that one is somehow less of an individual or certainly less spiritual, if what one does for financial support is not attuned to the 'true inner path.' We do not see any need for this kind of guilt or schism. You must see that one can have many elements of the self working in seemingly disparate ways, and yet, still be following a greater sense of a whole.

It is possible that at times in your life, all these aspects may come to a flow, and that your purpose or inner direction – all of your expression, can be put in one direction. But really, for most individuals, this does not occur. Judging the spiritual worth of jobs or professions can, unfortunately, lead to judgment. One does not want to devalue or undervalue people who are working in the many, many, many professions and jobs and activities that support such a complex world. Finding one's work spiritually fulfilling in many elements, and having financial success as well, is indeed one approach to feeling fulfillment in life. Yet, we would like to remind you again of the long view. The idea that a life and work and compensation must all be of a complete harmonious aspect is very recent. In other times one's work was inherited, one followed the mother's path, the father's path, the village's path, etc.

> Although it is a very positive ideal that one can
> integrate all aspects into a single working whole,
> it is but one option that may evolve or not.

We encourage you to allow yourself consideration of other ways of experiencing success and harmony. You can find yourself in a successful career that provides you income of a comfortable or considerable amount and harmoniously express your spirituality in other elements of your life. Recognizing the element of choice can eliminate the feeling of compromise. You can create the integration of your career skills and abilities and your spiritual aspects within yourself. The spiritual aspect of you is to be, we would hope, integrated. Open your images of what would make you happy, and evolve for yourself a way to do it.

> 'I want a new job!'
> Look again at your life as skills.
> Allow yourself to explore.

A class member asks for guidance, declaring, 'I want a new job!' When considering change, any change, hold first the idea of exploration. Play with and explore the idea that perhaps what you are looking for is not looking for you. Perhaps the images you are holding in your conscious mind are somehow not aligned with the energy of the inner self; therefore it is not coming into alignment. Alignment occurs when all the subtle elements connect as a whole.

We suggest looking through the paper at all the jobs, including ones you are totally not qualified for. Read all the job descriptions, just for fun, for exploration. Circle or in some way mark each one that somehow intrigues you. Make your choices from the inner self. 'This is funny. This intrigues me. I could never do it but...' Let that inner self bring information to you. Play with it. Put aside your specific focus and let yourself explore. There is a chance that in some section that you would never look at, because you are usually looking in the field of your expertise, there will be something very interesting, which will be amusing or intriguing to you. Look again at your life as skills, not just the skills you have been applying. If you see an interesting job, you have nothing to lose by writing a letter saying, 'Well, I don't actually have all the skills you require, but I can offer this...' You will discover that if a position intrigues you enough and alignment is present, you will be able to say with full strength what these wonderful qualities you have to share with them are.

Explore odd and unusual things or perhaps, mundane and ordinary things. Some may be jobs that you judge yourself by. 'Oh, I must be more than a clerk. I don't know why I'd want to choose that.' Perhaps that place of work is a place full of caring, supportive people. Perhaps you are in a time of your life where you do not need to have a great, expanded career-oriented position, but would flourish more in a steady, nurturing, less-demanding position. Here the inner self can guide you with wisdom toward linking you with that which you would not have consciously thought of. If you can still be playful, the next step is to follow through on some of these positions. If you do not follow through in reality by calling for interviews, etc., follow through in your thoughts. Look at why you chose a certain thing. Look at what really appealed to you. Consider what this information can tell you, show you or lead you to. Lay aside, if you can, the expectation of how it all must be. If this exploration becomes overwhelming, make an arbitrary choice. 'I'm going to choose this one.' You'll find when you do that you will either say, 'Yes, I am.' or 'No, I can't do that at all.' The energy will 'click' and reveal to you the direction to take.

Allow yourself to explore directions.
Consider choices not as right and wrong,
but as right and left!

If you create a job in this fashion, it will be wonderful for you to see how you can step out of expectations, even when your qualifications and credentials seem to lead you a certain way. What we are encouraging is to follow through with all the normal footwork of job hunting, sending resumes, etc., but allow also the unexpected, the something you have not even thought of, to come into your life. Let yourself think in terms of exploration! Consider choices not as right and wrong, but as right and left!

BALANCE IN WORKING WITH OTHERS

Finding your own balance is essential before you offer your energy to another.

Affirming balance of personality, of emotions, of physicality, is of prime importance to anyone, but especially those who work in the areas of counseling and health or in any situation with an orientation toward helping or healing. It is essential to offer energy as a clear energy source to be made use of by the other person in whatever way is best for them. Healing/Balancing work is a partnership of co-creation. It is a partnership that can work on many levels of awareness and comprehension. Thus, you must enter into the relationship trusting that the most expansive aspects of the self are the elements that will direct or orient the energy flow. You open together to the sense that you and your client, your friend, are drawing from knowledge and awareness and energy more than that which you know in only consciously learned ways.

Following this trusting of your connection with the All, it is especially important to be willing to release your *ideas* of the outcome. When you orient your work through the idea of Unity and the interconnection of all things, you invite in that very awareness. You may hold a certain idea, but again, be willing to let the All lead you. Remember, true healing and balancing may occur in ways that are other than alleviation of symptoms or elimination of a problem. There are many aspects to healing and many ways one can learn and grow through the process.

In assisting those suffering in the physical, we recommend strongly that you declare, with spoken intent, your energy as separate from those you assist.

It is also essential for those who are trying to assist in the balancing of others to be clear to themselves that to assist towards healing is *not* to absorb from another. It simply does not serve at all for one to absorb or receive disruptive, out of balance physical energy. The idea of healing where one directly absorbs energy with the idea of releasing it prevails and is tempting. It is very easy to overestimate your ability to release and balance. It is also useful to create practices and rituals which reflect releasing energy. An affirmation of clearing or releasing, combined with actual physical cleansing, as in washing your hands, is doubly beneficial. This creates an energetic and concrete clearing and cleansing and separating of energies. Taking on the difficulties of another will only limit your capacity to help them or yourself. When you are conscious in caring for your own energy, your balance helps you be available to continue to do so.

BALANCE IN INNER WORK

More important than health regimens are attitudes.

Balance can be found in many variations. We will not prescribe specific diets or regimens. We ask each of you to be sensitive to your understanding of your own balancing point and to recognize also that this balancing point can change. Any regime or ideas on one's health matters should be reviewed from time to time. A sensitivity and awareness towards the self is required. Your attitude will always be more important than any health regimen you undertake. Do not underestimate the value of repeated spoken affirmations and statements of intent towards balance, towards health. Your conscious mind is being continually educated to accept the increasing levels of awareness you reach out to. Like a child learning, the patterns you already carry and those held in the mass consciousness, are very strong and at times, stronger than the awareness you are now allowing to integrate. Thus reaffirming your understanding and intention is important. You will discover the way to do this as best suits you, be it affirmation, prayer, or symbol.

**No inner work can be accomplished in
an unbalanced state and you do well to honor
when it is not appropriate for you to work.**

As you choose to work on creative levels, as you choose to work spiritually in the mundane, balancing the physical and emotional, balancing through integration of awareness is the prime goal at all times. Balance is essential here. It is never useful to use words and energies of guilt when you sense you should not move forward or simply cannot move forward. Guilt is most often a reflection of ideas, not actuality. Do not berate the self. Honor the intelligence and wisdom telling you it is time to do nothing or to do things. In your goals you have high demands and expectations of self and this requires balance. It is fine to have ideals and desires of a high nature, but it will not serve if you are then driven to disregard the moments when you are out of balance for whatever reason. Out of balance is not a negative phrase. Being out of balance should not evoke guilt or self-recrimination. There are bodily rhythms affecting growth and activity beyond your emotional and psychological aspects.

The ideas of psychology are very beneficial, but unfortunately as a generation having been taught this perspective, one tends to see all things filtered through your own emotions. One tends to underestimate or disregard the cyclical rhythms of the body and the planet and other forces upon you. One tends to undervalue that there may actually be outside forces acting upon you. It is advisable to be more compassionate and forgiving, more understanding and gentle, toward yourselves. Struggle to keep as wide a perspective as possible. Honor the day that you simply want to stay in bed, as your saying goes.

Caretake yourself as best you can.

We are concerned that people are too demanding of themselves and insensitive to their own needs. People judge their own neediness. They are compassionate towards others, but often even among intimate friends and relationships, they are hesitant to reach out and ask for basic comforting and supporting, particularly on the visceral levels such as requiring physical hugging or embracing. We would like to encourage you to be able to move beyond this and ask for support. Allow an easy flow of support and affection to come to you. Although you may think of yourselves as fully supportive and affectionate, each of you know in your minds the times you were inhibited to ask and at the same time, would judge that what you would receive would be less *because* you had asked.

> Experiencing degrees of intimacy can be necessary
> for certain elements of movement
> in what is termed 'the spiritual path.'

It will be difficult to accept the levels of Unity that are available for merging with for those who are not yet ready to accept neediness within themselves, and physical contact in support of that neediness from those they are closest to. This is why experiencing degrees of intimacy can be necessary for movement and growth. As Unity consciousness comes more present, working with connection and others becomes more energized.

> Asking creates the link to All There Is.

We remind you also, in your times of need, you can call upon Unity feelings from energies outside of yourselves, such as your guides, such as whatever energy source you wish to touch into. Each of you is fully capable of receptivity and linking with such energy sources. It can be in the manner you desire: visual communications, verbal sensations, experiential or subtle awareness. You are the initiator of the connection.

> Each of you is fully capable of receptivity
> and linking with energy sources.
> You are the initiator of the connection.

CHAPTER EIGHT

ESOTERICA

PAST LIVES – OTHER LIVES

We see each life expression
as unto itself, having the full right to create from itself,
to choose its own experience, to make upon its own foundations.

On the idea of past lives, we use the term 'other life expressions' rather than past lives, since we do not see the time as simply of the past. Although we do not deny that there is an experience structure such as linear time, it is not as simple and direct as perceived, as reflected in the concept of the space-time continuum. Yet, we do not see the concept of linear time as totally invalidated or as existing only as a thought-construct, as some contend. There is validity to the concept of linear time and it holds influence beyond being simply a thought-construct. It is appropriate to use the concept of linear time when thinking of other life expressions. Linear time carries within itself an inherent energy pulsation of the essence of Being. The fullness of time is a complex web of time, space and energy.

In this context, life expressions – present, past, future, other – are not only in a linear time, following one upon the other, but in a circular time-frame that is a continuum. This continuum is linear in one sense and yet, also holds life as an all occurring-at-once concept. Consider the image of a wooden wheel. See the hub of the wheel as being the Core Energy, which some call the soul. Radiating off from the hub are the spokes of the wheel which represent other life expressions. We caution you, though, to not see everything in the past as over and done with. Or in the future, as not having occurred. Continue to hold the idea that somehow these other life expressions are pulsating with and existing concurrently with this present. It is at the core essence that there is an awareness, a full experiential consciousness of all these diverse elements.

We see what is thought of as the choice of life expression as a complex interconnection of goals, intents and desires of focus. We see these life expressions – your past lives, your future lives – as interconnected and bonded by the matrix but, in essence, separate. In this, each life expression has the full right to be unto itself individually. Each life expression bears full right to have awareness and understanding of all the other life aspects of the greater self, but also has full right to have the choices of an individual life be made based solely upon the opportunities and needs of that individual and specific life expression's energy field.

This present life reality is where your focus and responsibility lie.

Let us also say that the life expression you are presently in, the one you are fully participating in now, is the one of your concern and focus, the one you are responsible to. There are those who are very easily able to transcend the physical form and feel great alignment with other lives, other elements of all that you are. But one must do this always with great balance and acknowledgement that this present life reality is where your focus and responsibility lie. It is also where your love and affinity and affection lie.

ANOTHER VIEW ON REINCARNATION & KARMA

We do not hold the idea that one is destined to act upon Actions caused by another aspect of self.

On reincarnation in general, we hold the idea that there is an essence of the being that explores life in form and that this essence has a core of self-knowing that generates life expressions – what you call lifetimes. Knowledge and experiences of the life expressions are known and added to the knowingness of the core.

We do not hold the customarily understood idea of an inviolable cumulative aspect of reincarnation in which each life expression is ordained to be a reflection of what came before and that one is destined to act out debts or come to peace with unresolved issues. We do not hold to the view of karma as a great cumulative weight upon a being and that all that you were before and all that you will be comes to play in definite finality within each aspect of yourself in a relentless mode.

Although the matrix of a being does carry the vibrations of what has gone before, or in the future, we do not see that there is any *compelled* charge placed upon a life expression to act out or modify or express the energies from any other life expression. Many people who have come to an understanding of a concept of reincarnation desire conscious awareness and exploration of these other aspects of themselves. One can use these understandings for further awareness of the present life. Perhaps one can come to understand how motivations of another life expression are possibly influencing choices made in the present. We do not hold the idea of *destiny*, that one is destined to act upon actions caused by another aspect of self.

We see each individual as fully capable of and responsible for synthesizing their own belief structure.

We understand this presents, perhaps, a differing view on the nature of reincarnation and karma. We are not trying to convince anyone of one view or the other. Rather, we are hoping to present to you another way of looking at it; another understanding. We see each individual as fully capable of and responsible for synthesizing their own belief structure. We ask only that you use your inner wisdom, your inner core as your guide.

We hold that the growth and structure of the present life expression is not inexorably dependent upon aligning with another person or element from another time or aspect.

The idea of each life expression having a right to be unto itself is not to say that you may not bring into your lives what you have known before or those you had connections with. This is not to say that situations may not come about that are similar or reflections of other times. There may be reflections of other lives coming into the present one. All of this is interaction between aspects of the whole, and an interaction that is a reflection of choice. Living involves elements of choice and, indeed, you may choose to realign with many an individual, or re-explore a situation, or balance a pattern of action. But, again, we hold that the growth and structure of the present life expression is not inexorably dependent upon aligning with another person or element from another time or aspect.

No life is dependent upon its alignment with another life or with people from those lives.

We also do not accept the idea of destined karmic bonds that cannot be healed or broken. We are not saying you will not find an individual that you are very much aligned to. This can be. You may have shared other life expressions with a specific person or group of people or an element thereof, over and over again. Yet, no life is dependent upon its alignment with another life or with people from those lives. We do not see any great cosmic, celestially-coordinated dependency. These influences may be experienced, yes. These influences may be felt, may act as a motivator of action. But we do not see it as a cosmic morality that these balances must be brought about. Our view is that each life expression has the right, and we see, the *responsibility,* to create unto itself.

We see it as interference when energy from another life expression causes choice and action below the conscious awareness level of an individual. We have assisted people to close such energy flow into the visceral elements of the body from other life expressions, and to instead, enhance conscious knowledge and awareness. This facilitates one coming into an understanding of the motivations or difficulties of expansion, rather than experiencing interference. There can be awareness of the whole of ones self, awareness of the interactions between the many aspects of ones self, but this is very different from having your choices preformed and directed.

There are a mélange of influences that touch into the growth of each life.
The evolution of a lifetime is not following a cosmic script.

Lives are generated with certain precepts, with certain capabilities, perhaps; with certain focuses. Lives as they are lived, are on-going moments of creation, co-creation and creativity. Portions of life are created by the present conscious life self and other portions are co-created with the essence of the soul, the essence, perhaps, of influences of other life expressions, and the essences of connections with other forms – guides, teachers, etc. Thus, a mélange of influences touch into the growth of each life.

The evolution of a lifetime is not following a cosmic script. Also, if the direction or the outcome is not met as first focused on, there is no judgment on the life. A willingness to release the final outcome, to allow the outcome to come to its own evolution, is how a life moves on. It is true that one might bring into a present reality certain attributes, qualities, ideas or aspects you wish to explore or discover and perhaps balance. Again, we do not see this as an ordained mantle of accountability, but rather as a choice of exploration.

In our perspective, we do not hold the idea that is often expressed in the term 'karma,' that everything is geared towards a hierarchical rising growth pattern from low to high, and that there are lessons and retribution, punishments and balancing etc., brought upon the lives. There is no ordained, final outcome awaiting you. Directions may be set, patterns may be in place but if, in the web of all the interconnections, the outcome, which was once perceived a certain way, begins to shift, that is in harmony and balance. There are times when individuals have very strong focuses, which seem to indicate the pull of destiny. There are lives that seem as if they must follow a certain alignment. This is true. But, it is still not a reflection of a cosmic creation. It is actually more a reflection of acute awareness and receptivity within an individual in a present life to the vibrations of those patterns, talents and opportunities available to them.

EXPLORING OTHER LIVES

Awareness of other life expressions you have participated in can add to the consciousness of your present self, and can add to the whole of your being.

When you have a sense there is information from other lives that might serve you, this is something you can explore. We suggest you explore these things in the awareness level, as you would explore another culture. You want to have knowledge, awareness of other life expressions you have participated in, to add to the consciousness of your present self, to add to the whole of your being.

Allow yourself to recognize information coming to you. Allow yourself to consider that there can be validity in the information.

You can begin the process of allowing information to flow to you by stating your intent, by energizing the idea that you can receive such awareness; by simply making the statement, 'I am receptive to awareness.' We see this as a natural way of receiving information. The information may come through dreaming. It may come in reading books and recognizing a situation. In films. In other people. The process is allowing yourself to recognize this information coming to you, and allowing yourself to consider that there can be validity in the information. Honoring the validity of such information continues to be a challenge for most people. We encourage you to allow information to come to you. When you recognize it, or when you allow yourself to recognize it, we encourage you to allow yourself to accept that the information can indeed be valid. The information may be allegorical. It may be as metaphor. But we feel you will be able to glean some element of information that will have meaning to you.

In the dream state, images from another life expression are often overlaid with present interpretations. Information that is difficult for the conscious mind to comprehend is formed into symbols that are more comprehensible. This is another natural processing of receiving information which is basically coded in symbols or allegory or information which is unknown to or outside any of your current experience or understanding. This is not to say information received in dreams or meditation as coded elements is inaccurate. The essence of the meaning is where the validity lies.

Separation of the energies experienced within the body
as emotional contact with or empathic response to other life
expressions can lead to clarity of understanding.

Many individuals go to others, such as astrologers, oracular readers and the like, for assistance in clarifying their sense that they are being motivated and influenced in some way by other lives. It is an accurate perception that many human beings are being influenced on unconscious levels by energies flowing to them and within them from other life expressions. Energy that flows into a person's form in which knowledge is blocked from or not received by the conscious mind can cause difficulty, blockage, and impediment. Indeed, much other life expression information is blocked from the conscious mind. Information that is able to flow through the inner awareness levels and comes forth in the method of dreaming, meditations and the like, is often dismissed or incorrectly interpreted. At times when a person focuses an intent to explore other lives, a connection is made and information more easily flows and becomes available to the now-receptive conscious mind.

In our view, the most efficient way of making use of information and demonstrations from other life expressions is from a distance as an observer. Such exploration should not involve your physical being or the emotions of the physical being. It is not essential for growth and development to be buffeted, as it were, by other life expressions. The idea of pain, karmic debt, acting out karmic relationships is not necessary for total experience of this current life expression. Rather, certain awareness is brought forward and integrated into the being.

Although the individual is certainly part of and connected with an aspect of all the other life expressions that are generated from the soul impetus, it does not mean that they are blended as one. Again, we see each individual being as entitled to create that one life fully in their own flow of energy and according to precepts that they bring forth in the present. It is possible for one to learn from other aspects of self without having it as an emotional block or on an experiential level. When past life information does come forward from whatever source, use the information as a tool to separate this life expression from that other. Use the information to lift the feelings of another time which interfere with your present chosen work or path out of your current life expression.

AN AFFIRMATION FOR EXPLORING PAST LIVES

I energize and declare my right to determine the path of my being in this present realization without emotional fears, desires, antipathies, pain, physical limitation and the like, from other aspects of the self's soul.

I permit awareness to come present and ask information, guidance, understanding, awareness, joy, journey, awareness of all the beings that a soul may encompass to flow easily.

But I ask that this awareness not come through the physical being, that it not come without conscious understanding or the ability to garner such understanding. I ask awareness to not come in any interfering manner.

This is an affirmation that could easily be spoken and created by any of you. This affirmation embodies the essence of the principles we recommend to anyone choosing to consciously explore life expressions.

Bleed-through occurs when energy from another life expression links with you in your present life expression and therefore causes imbalance in your system.

We would like to address the importance and relevance of the past life/other life connection to the physical health of the body. There are often occasions when the physical form, the body, links with past lives, future lives (you see why we then say, other life expressions!) and through this linking has energy flow that can move from one form to another and can bring change, perhaps experienced as imbalance, in the present. Imbalances in the form that come from other life expressions work on subtle levels because it is not clear to the individual what element of their make-up is creating this imbalance. We are particularly referring to illness, dis-ease, accidents, breakages of the bones, etc. We call this aspect bleed-through – when energy from another life expression links with you in your present life expression and therefore causes imbalance in your system. In most instances of bleed-through, there is a connection, as in, an energy linking with some emotional or situational experience that the two life expressions share. It is that blending together of the energies, the two aspects of a whole in different places in time, sharing a moment of energy similarity, which allows and creates this link of energy.

Bleed-through can also be the root in situations where an individual cannot come to grips with the situation or come to an understanding of their own motivations. In such cases, it may be that the root energy and the information presented by that energy, is literally not of the individual's make-up. It is not in that individual's sub-conscious, in the psychological term. It simply is not accessible to the individual's awareness.

Bleed-through can be imaged as having made a link on a psychic level with another aspect of self.

Such a link allows a flow-through, as in osmosis, of energy. Difficulty ensues because the energy is being drawn, through empathy or sympathy, into their physical form but the information may be unrecognizable. Thus, it cannot be processed by the conscious mind or the emotions of the being, as it is energy outside of self. Very often in these situations, if one is cognizant of some spiritual terms and concepts, individuals will get a sense and they will say, 'Oh maybe this is a past life connection.' Such recognition is the Inner Awareness sensing the vibrations and bringing the idea to the conscious mind. You may wonder how one can determine if an influence is indeed such a past life sensing. Return to the inner wisdom. Use your conscious mind, your ally, to express the idea.

Physically re-experiencing another life aspect is not necessary, and does not promote development or growth.

One idea is that you could process this type of awareness, perhaps through what is called regression, where you bring up or experience other life awareness as much as possible. In our view, the awareness is certainly usable and applicable, but the physicality – the emotions, the manifestation of illness or disease or emotional swings – a desire to *physically* re-experience another life aspect, is not necessary and does not promote development or growth.

A sealing is an affirmation that the present individual life has full rights to its own creativity and own creation.

To help counter-balance interference from bleed-through energy, we have often assisted individuals with something we call a sealing, as in sealing-off of the energy of the other life expression. It is really an affirmation that one's present individual life has full rights to its own creativity and own creation. In an affirmation for sealing, we always energize that full information and awareness of the other life expression can come to the conscious mind and be remembered and understood and made use of by the individual. But, we energize that the interfering visceral level of absorption cease. Such an affirmation facilitates a lifting of certain fears and discomfort. When the physical absorption is halted, it is then easier to use the conscious mind in the understanding of the concept. You can explore other life expressions but, again, we strongly recommend you do so from the observer viewpoint, rather than an absorption level.

Often the life expressions one taps into are those in distress or difficulty. It is that part of you linked to your core matrix that senses the strong vibration of need in this other aspect of yourself. Absorbing these vibrations into your physical form is not the way to serve this other aspect. It is more helpful if, when you get conscious awareness, you then are able – with your conscious mind, in integration with all of yourself – to send caring energy and affirmations to this other aspect of self. You may act as a director, a channeler of healing energy, but always consciously affirming that the energy is available to be used by the other as they most need to, rather than in a fashion directed by you.

SOUL MATES & SOUL/ESSENCE GROUPS

We do not hold to the concept of soul mate,
although there may indeed be chosen reconnection with another.

There is so much mutability in existence, we cannot hold to the idea that there would be only a singular person or energy that one would have an unbreakable destiny to be with. We do not see that any part of the growth of a life expression would be in abeyance while an individual awaited the unity with a destined mate or partner. There are indeed individuals who choose to have reconnection with another or others one has shared with from many other life expressions. The option of such chosen reconnection exists. But we do not accept singularity. We do not accept immutable destiny. Each life expression is an evolution. Life is not patterned out before you. Life is created, it is active. A person may experience what you would call a destiny – a very strong focus that again and again pulls and focuses and draws – but it is really a very rare person who cannot create or discover another choice.

**Soul or Essence groups reflect an element of you
connected very strongly to another life expression,
or perhaps to another reality.**

It is not an easy task to be one who is breaking or stretching, perhaps, some of the roles of your own present society. For some of you, the reasons you are drawn to this are connected with the idea of soul or essence groups. Here, soul and essence refers to a deep sensing of the core elements of being that can carry the capacity for continuing connection. The idea of groups connected at the deepest continuing aspect of being reflects an element of yourself connected very strongly to another life expression, perhaps even another reality different from this one. Awareness of such connections can give one a unique perspective, as the traveler living in another country often can step aside and be somewhat objective about the mores of the visited society. Thus, the support of the soul group connection and memory can support spiritual pioneering. Yet, a strong inner linking or awareness of these connections can also lead to feeling not connected to society or even reality, feelings of being an outsider or different.

Energizing the idea of soul/essence groupings through conscious awareness also acts as a magnet, if you will, for recognition of the other elements of such groups. There are other levels where individuals come together, just as in your reality, with certain connections of energy. Such group connections very often remain in these energy levels. One does not always re-connect in your daily reality with the people you are sharing a soul/essence connection with. But, when you feel a bonding, or a comfort level, or an intimacy which seems somehow immediate or not directly based on the actual present experience, it may indeed reflect a connection in form with a member of a soul group. Allowing recognition and consideration of this possibility honors a touching through the interconnections of the Web.

In other times, individual exploration of different soul/essence connections, different aspects of the self, was much more subtly experienced and recognized.

Experiencing such interconnections, as with the soul/essence group, is a natural movement, a natural flow of the energy. More and more individuals are experiencing and exploring recognition and awareness of all the elements they may be part of and participating in. In addition, the very concept of the possibility of being more than your physical body and mind is supported in today's culture. There is a literal freedom in the sociological structure and political system of your time, to explore radically different elements within a lifetime. Although you may be quick to recognize the imperfections within your system, remember this reality operates much in the realm of paradox.

144

In other times, individual exploration of different soul/essence connections and different aspects of the self, was much more subtly experienced and recognized. Individuals were required to have a particular focus – a trade, a craft, a role assigned for life. Social units stayed together for longer and more consistent periods, and one's role within them was more defined and prescribed. When the stranger came to town, it was not just a stranger that the people would react to; it really was that that persons energy was experienced as not linked, in many a case, to a very, very strong soul grouping energy.

Individual exploration is, in part,
a reflection of the creativity of your time.

Other cultures and societies at different times have experienced freedom of exploration. But it is more so in this country, in this time and in other countries which afford such options for the individual. Thus, you find support to be open to explore philosophy and practices of far different cultures and environments. You find yourself open to explore other realms of being, to allow the sense of touching into different vibrations of consciousness and more.

GUIDES & GUIDANCE

There are beings far removed from a commitment to a certain societal level of existence - these are perceived as guides.

There are ones that are described as angelic, although we would not choose to use this term, but would describe them rather as being far removed from a commitment to a certain societal level of existence. It is such energies, intelligences, arenas of consciousness that are experienced and perceived as personal or individual guides. Many such guides are, in fact, very close to your physical existence and that is why many of them have specific personalities and can recall or describe themselves by life expressions they have been. Many of these teacher-guides serve in the realm of presenting information of a factual nature to individuals, and this information is received in a form of channeling. It is not the same as permitting an occupation of the body, but it is mostly a transmitting phenomenon from one aspect of reality to another.

The first step is to expand the parameters of the conscious mind to have some working idea of the concept of Guides. An individual can prepare for this receptivity by allowing the conscious consideration that there can be such intelligences and that teachers, helpers and guides are available. For many of you this is already a given concept. For others, consider the possibility of exchange with intelligence in another realm of being and see where such consideration can lead you.

> We caution you to not have rigid images
> of how these teachers can present
> themselves or what they must be.

In the same vein of allowing the consideration of guides, can we caution you not to have rigid images of how these teachers can present themselves or what they must be? The current image of guides is indeed an *image* and it is very much a creation of your own time and society. In reading history or mythology, one can see many other presentations, other forms, other experiences of guide energies. It is more comfortable for a contemporary individual to feel that the spirit of a great doctor has come to guide one with health information than it is to have a dog-headed god appear to give information. But you can see that the information could indeed be coming from the same source. It is rather a choice of what images are comfortable for a society and its people. Guides create forms, linked with the reality of the receiver, geared toward acceptance of the experience.

This is why we caution you to not hold to rigid, specific images. Begin with these images, but if your own experience is somewhat different or beyond what you first expected, we encourage you to be able to permit yourself to experience some of what does occur.

> When you are opening to other energy systems,
> it is your responsibility to direct, delineate, and
> define the system or manner of exchange.

It is a misunderstanding that one must be *all* open and receptive or one will not support reception. A clear, defined agreement will serve you well. Again, you have the right and responsibility to define your experience. As an example, it is essential to maintain body balance, thus you do not want your sleep state constantly disturbed. You do not want physical reactions to the exchange. You do not want to enter a receptive mode while driving, for example. All these elements are for your consideration.

Ideas of an agreement of interaction can become clear to you. Do not give the mantle of responsibility to beings who may not be omniscient, who may not have full cognition of the needs of your reality. Perhaps you can create a comfortable working format, as in the simple phrases, 'I am open to receptivity and I am closed to receptivity.' We suggest you write down, empower and energize this agreement; this statement of your intent. Form a symbol or icon of this agreement which will hold the vibration of all you have created. As an example, you can create that when you hold an image of a crystal or an actual crystal, you are initiating and welcoming receptivity.

There is an energy on the planet
supporting interaction and exchange.

Do not hold the fear that you will lose connection with your guide through this kind of accountability. You will not. Rather, you are embracing the element of interaction. It is no longer a time of passive receptivity of guidance and teachings only. There is now an energy supporting interaction and exchange. Such interaction must be embraced with your willingness to be accountable and responsible.

One of the great ways to limit expansion is
to hone in immediately on defining an experience,
its outcome, and how it must be used.

A lecture participant shares, 'I have been able to get some material in which it seems as if I am channeling, but I am not sure because perhaps one possibility is that I am channeling and the other is that it comes from my subconscious...' Here, the ideas of such experiences are defining the actuality of the moment. In a practical, goal and outcome-oriented culture it is a challenge for you to allow yourself to be free-form about activities or time. It is a challenge to let experience lead you.

Remember, one can channel or receive in myriad ways. Channeling is simply bringing an energy flow through pathways referred to as channels. This energy may not be avatars. It can be a flow of energy itself, as from Nature. It can be connections with elements. It can be other planetary energies. Channeling can be connection to an inner-self, the unconscious self, past selves, future selves, etc. We offer all of these myriad choices to purposefully confuse you. If you cannot immediately define what it is, and if the experience and information feels positive and meaningful to you, perhaps by knowing there are many possible explanations, you will permit yourself to allow a period of exploration.

Again, when people do not perceive their spirituality in the long haul, they are drawn to spiritual mountain climbing. They want to capture the experience, label it, wrap it up in a box and have it. This attitude of immediate concrete definition limits the allowing and permitting of exploration.

ANOTHER VIEW ON EARTH CHANGES

**We do not see a great cosmically-induced or created,
moral correction to be brought forth on the planet Earth.**

There is a continuing idea that a great destructive element, a punishing element particularly concerning the planet Earth, is present in the Universe, which will bring great destruction through natural means as well as through warfare onto the planet. It is further held that this is a cosmically ordained premise. There are many individuals who are, in fact, preparing for this time: some in an actual physical sense by storing food, buying isolated patches of land, etc., and others by directing emotional and psychic energies toward the alleviation of such a situation.

We would never declare that our view is the totality or the Truth or in any way a finite statement on anything that we see. Yet, we must strongly say we do not hold to such ideas of cosmic corrections or punishments through cataclysmic realities. There may be at some time physical upheavals and changes which may reflect a natural pattern of the Earth simply lost in the mists of time and therefore unknown as part of a natural flow. This is also not to say that there will not be destruction by warfare or other human-created catastrophes. But we do not see any such occurrence as a sense of judgment. Our experience of the Source of energy is of one that does not respond in judgment to specific moralities. Such moralities are more a reflection of society, social mores, and customs, than directives from Source.

*Humankind is capable of living in a creative way;
expanding and changing its relationships
through its growing and evolving perceptions.*

If you look at your own planet in historical perspective, you can see how hard and fast rules of humankind's behavior have changed, vacillated, and have been in opposition over history. If you look with a long perspective at your planet, you will see that the human beings and the societies created by them are fully capable of evolving myriad ways of relating to the universe. This capacity to develop and expand, to transcend and include what came before, to integrate and evolve differently in the future is indeed the uniqueness of humankind.

*Choose to work toward your ideas of peace or harmony in a way
that is an expression of your own individual spiritual impulse.*

We are also asked, 'About the war and peace issue, with the possibility of human-made catastrophes of war, what kind of peace work do you see as being most effective on the part of ordinary citizens, people not in elected office?' Here your true option is to work toward your ideas of peace or harmony in a way that is an expression of your own individual spiritual impulse. Allow the Inner Awareness to open a path of such service. There is strength and power in energy and direction aligned through the inner self.

You must understand, though, that peace or specific images of what that entails, is not a universally accepted idea on your planet. One must accept the idea that there are other individuals who feel that war, in their countries, is truly what they are fully aligned to from their deepest aspects. Again, the expression of paradox and duality of your reality is a challenge. It is not our intention, though, to be negative and to tell you that you cannot generate good or harmony or balance by holding the ideal and working for this ideal. Each note in the symphony holds power and import, and an individual's actions and choices can create and bring harmony. Rather, we remind you to accept the existence of paradox to support you when you become overwhelmed by the seeming results of its existence.

OUTER SPACE & PERSONAL EXPLORATION

Although most people cannot travel in outer space, individuals try to step out of their own parameters to soften the input of the density of form, and allow heightened awareness.

Let us close this section with thoughts on the idea of expansion and the ability to step out of the bounds of paradox. A lecture participant tells us, 'I was reading a book by a former Apollo astronaut in which he describes his experiences in space as the astronauts having their minds open to looking at our planet differently or themselves differently, countries differently, whether they wanted to or not. It just happened. What makes outer space so unique that those kinds of experiences occur, as compared to our earth-bound experiences?'

Such expanded awareness experiences in space are supported by the literal disconnection from the parameters of the everyday physical reality of Earth. Even though the astronauts are still bound in their body, their capsule and attire, this profound sense of difference expands the visceral sense of the parameters of being. The conscious mind also had permission to literally be in the unknown and this can support a great influx of awareness from the inner senses. So in a profound way, an individual can open to the deepest knowing that they are more than the physical body and how they have understood the physical parameters of reality. This idea is the very cornerstone of expansion.

If you yourself can allow just the consideration that there is more than your physical reality, the wonderful tool of the conscious mind is then quite capable of extrapolating upon and expanding understandings, belief systems, etc. Separation from the energy of the planet and from the mass consciousness in actual physical distance enhances inner permission to recognize more than physical reality. The mythologies of space, of heaven, of other levels, of other planets, etc.- all of expansion - whether one consciously holds such beliefs or not, come into play in the Inner Awareness as well, adding a structure for the conscious mind to permit a broader perspective.

All these elements come together in the unique environment of outer space. Only a handful of people have the opportunity of this atmosphere, and this uniqueness also adds to such a catharsis of awareness. The unique aspect of the situation supports allowing and permitting such unique experiences. Although most people cannot travel in space, individuals try to step out of their own parameters in many ways. In their meditations, in the water tanks, in being in the ocean itself, etc. All of these approaches are ways to soften the input of the energy and density of form, and allow the heightening of awareness. There is a receptivity level that really is going on all the time. But since you've decided to participate in form, you cannot be extended in receptivity at all times and still be in form.

This is why we address integration again and again. Life is not an either/or proposition. It is a moment here, a moment there. Expanded then focused or both at once. Movement followed by plateau. Allow yourselves to move out of the images of polarity. Polarity is reflected in almost all of your nature and it is a real challenge to hold the idea of many things occurring at once. Holding the concept of only one or the other is such a limitation. Life is many things. A bit. A touch. A movement. A flow.

> In your searching, in your quests for yourself,
> your greatest contribution is that you share the
> energy of 'I seek to understand' with so many.
> This energy pulsates about you, the searcher,
> even if you do not share it verbally and directly.

In closing, we thank you. We honor you. If we can give you anything, we would most like to leave with you a strong idea, a strong concept to use as an anchor, a root of support. It is simply that you do have wisdom within you. There is guidance within you. There is a link within you that can direct you, lead you, call you, and move with you to certain paths, certain choices, certain awareness, to certain knowledge.

We thank you for honoring the impulse, the sense within that allowed you to consider material such as ours. We honor that because it represents the element of the explorer. You have allowed yourself to step outside of everyday reality and to engage in a consideration of ideas outside your everyday methods of perceiving.

There is the unseen world. The web of interconnection is not to be experienced with only the eyes and the ears. Much of what we are about in our sharing is encouraging people to explore working with elements that are not experienced in the everyday channels. By giving validity to sensing, you can touch into a knowingness of more than you can readily perceive. We very much want to encourage elements of consideration and exploration. Each of you has the ability, through many means, to experience and know information beyond the usual ways of sensing and knowing. We honor you in your willingness to explore these abilities.

> We encourage elements of
> consideration and exploration.
> We encourage the idea that
> there can be more
> to understanding, to knowledge,
> than that which is
> readily perceived.

COMING TO ORION
OPENING TO CHANNEL

FROM THE FIRST EDITION

Channeling moved into my life swiftly, yet gently, at a time when I was open and aware of the idea that you are more than your physical body. The initial experience was not overwhelming or dramatic, but rather, acceptance of an opportunity.

In retrospect, the antecedents, the guideposts leading to this work were clearly marked. I had long been interested in exploring the nature of reality, the meaning of things. My first directions took me through the study of the human experience: I explored psychology, sociology, anthropology and archaeology. From these studies and life itself, I moved to further paths of awareness, towards the metaphysical, the esoteric. My interests touched upon, absorbed and integrated many aspects and this exploration was also supported by the era I was living in. As a portent of the Orion work, my thrust always was one of integration. My life was a weaving of many elements.

In the mid-seventies I came to know the works of Seth, channeled through Jane Roberts. I was exposed earlier to the idea of channeling with the Edgar Cayce information, the Alice Bailey books and others, but 'The Seth Material' connected strongly for me, as it did for so many. Spirituality became a continuing element of my life, but not a main focus or dominant theme.

1979 found me pregnant, living in rural Central Virginia with my husband, Perry, working in stained glass and commuting to Charlottesville once a week to take a course in ESP Awareness. During these classes I discovered I was very receptive, but not as adept in sending. During each class session I would find myself doodling in my notebook, circles and scrolls, in a rather compulsive manner. I simply couldn't stop and if I let my attention wander from the doodling, my hand would move freely across the page. Of course, I asked the teacher, a local psychic, what she felt this experience was. She felt I was connecting with the energy of my unborn child. I was quite attracted to these doodles and although I couldn't discover any meaning in them, I kept them and, in fact, literally filed them away. Almost two years later, when I had what I knew was a channeling experience, I looked again at those doodles. Looking at them with the idea of channeling through writing in my thoughts, I could easily see letters and words within the circles and scrolls. A connection had been made, but I was not yet open to recognizing it.

In the summer of 1981, 1 met an interesting and friendly couple who eventually told me of the work of Robert Monroe and their involvement with him. Robert Monroe had written an excellent book, *Journeys Out of Body*, in which he chronicles his experiences and growing awareness from those experiences.

He later founded The Monroe Institute, located in Faber, Virginia. In its literature, the Institute states its research division conducts ongoing studies in enhancement of human consciousness and the development of methods and techniques which may result in practical use thereof. One of the practical applications of their research is a series of audiotapes using nonverbal audio patterns to create a state of both brain hemispheres acting and working together simultaneously. This process is called 'Hemispheric Synchronization' or Hemi-Sync.™

I was drawn to the book, I was drawn to my new friends, and soon I ordered a set of the Hemi-Sync tapes, called The Discovery series™. I began working with the tapes and found it a unique, opening experience. But it was difficult finding time away from my now toddling son, the renovation of our house and life in general, to devote time to being in an altered state exploring other levels of being. Everyday life called too strongly, and because of the difficulties of finding time for this exploration, I finally decided to participate in the Gateway Voyage™, a six-day, intensive program held in a retreat atmosphere at The Monroe Institute. This decision was the catalyst toward choices that eventually led my life in another direction.

My days at the Gateway held three major events for me. First, I met and became close friends with three very special people. We shared some intense and magical moments then and since. The bond we established then is still present within us and links us. Secondly, I had an experience with channeling through writing, which at the time

I referred to as automatic writing. Lastly, I had a full trance voice channeling experience. Do let me be clear that these events were my unique, personal experience of the Gateway Voyage

The Gateway program, in general, is oriented toward personal expansion, and this is how I opened and explored within the Gateway structure. I found myself as part of a group of individuals, all of whom were ready and willing to allow themselves to explore, who accepted the basic premise that 'you are more than your physical body.' We were guided and assisted by experienced and caring staff people. We were in a beautiful natural environment and our every day lives and cares were far away. In addition, I had in the very beginning already connected strongly with my three new friends. Eventually, because we were always together, we were known as 'The Quartet'. In this safe, nurturing place, I experienced my unique encounters and discoveries as part of a comfortable expansion.

The retreat structure was such that we listened to the Hemi-Sync tapes individually in our rooms, meeting afterwards as a group to discuss and share our experiences. In an early tape, we were guided toward some visualization. I always had little success visualizing and this time was no exception. My thoughts drifted to what I knew of a stressful element between two of my new friends.

I found myself thinking, 'If there is any way I can help, if there is any information I can receive that would help them, I'm willing to receive it.' In swift response to my willingness to be open, to receive, my mind filled with words of information. Some of it referred to past life connections, some to dynamics between them. In any event, I had indeed received information. Afterwards, I tentatively approached them and asked if they were interested in some of the information I had received during the visualizing tape. They were, and indeed, the information was meaningful to them in ways it had not for me.

To be honest, the rest of my experience at the Gateway was mostly directed from, what I would now call, my Inner Awareness. The Hemi Sync tapes usually had a certain structure or guided aspect directed toward specific kinds of experience. After the first experience, I often used the tapes in my own way, not always participating with the guided directions. I hadn't consciously planned to create my own Gateway, but I trusted and followed my inner sense. I reconnected again and again with that source of information and asked questions of it, had dialogues with it.

Later in the week, while listening to a tape with the whole group, I began the same kind of compulsive doodling as I had almost two years before in the ESP class. This time, though, I had a sense that the doodles were a kind of connection. I closed my eyes, and said, 'Is someone there?' Slowly, my hand wrote in a large loopy stroke, 'Yes.' I was not fearful of this connection. The Gateway Voyage program taught me about using clearly stated affirmations in all my explorations. I felt protected by the Gateway affirmation for connecting only with energy equal to or higher than my own.

I got the attention of my friend as to what was going on with me and a few of us went off to explore this connection. One person asked questions and I opened and allowed the answers to flow through. I could almost physically sense a flow of energy, akin to a slight electrical current, flow down my right arm and onto the page. The words flowed together. I was writing in a very large, sprawling script, with no spaces, no dotting of i's or crossing of t's, which flowed over large pieces of drawing paper. Afterwards, we went through and drew lines to separate the words.

It appeared that I had connected to the energy of a small boy named Jeff, who said he was eight years old. He described an intensely burning house – his own house with his parents still inside. He said he had gone into the house to find his parents, but when he did there was nothing but blackness. He was very frightened in this blackness. He said he had seen my 'color' and that was why he called out to me, and then, he heard me answer him and found he was able to talk to me. This reception was indeed a unique experience, but it was not frightening, uncomfortable or draining. Rather, it was a special feeling of connection. It was like those special moments when you connect to nature or to an animal in a way that transcends the everyday world of being a human being. Jeff was to return and be part of my life for almost a year sharing guidance through channeled-writing.

Somewhere in the course of the days at the Gateway, the inner voice of guidance talked with me about the possibility of channeling. I was told I had the physical ability to work as a channel, that this was an inherent ability, chosen before birth. The ability was present, but the choice to act as a channel was to be a conscious one made by me in my present reality. After a moment (or so it seems!), I said I was willing to work in this way, but I had one request. I did not want to give up hours of my life in an altered state with no memory of what occurred. Thus, intuitively, I accepted the mantle and the responsibility of cognizance.

Years later, when I began to work with Orion, they talked of this gut level decision of mine. Orion said it was a symbol of integration, that my desire to be cognizant represented the idea that a channel would work with the energies channeled, not only as a receiver but also as one able to experience and work with the information in a present way. Later, Orion shared that this very willingness to be present was a quality Orion was aligned to and waiting for. In retrospect, I an also see how the cognizance factor led to my being immersed in the Orion perspectives in a complex conscious and non-conscious manner with a kind of vitality and immediacy of presence.

Towards the end of the Gateway program I had one more experience. One evening when everyone was having free time one of the Quartet and I sequestered ourselves in our room. I remember feeling a heaviness in my body and then the awkwardness of having my jaw and mouth manipulated. It was a disconcerting experience. I had asked for cognizance and this was not the same feeling as being conscious. Being cognizant is understanding the words spoken, but as if they are heard at a distance or as an echo.

I spoke slowly, softly and not very clearly. Afterwards I was very tired, very drained. Again, I had the sensation of a separate and distinct current of energy flowing through my body. Although the event itself moved slowly, I felt tired as if I had done something doubly fast. I felt a kind of awkwardness, a disconcerting feeling about the whole experience. Part of it came from the fact that many people found this trance-channeling too odd, too much a step into another reality, and I was not ready to stand out that much from others. Channeling through writing was somewhat private. Full trance channeling was more public, more known. In fact, it would be over a year before I voice channeled again, with a try or two along the way, and then came the connection with Orion, and what would become a major thrust of my life. I left the Gateway with new friends and new experiences in my life. The experiences continued and at one point I called the Institute to talk with someone. Bob Monroe gave me the excellent advice to act as an observer, maintain a notebook of my experiences and stay aware.

Several weeks after the Gateway, I sat down with a pen and paper and opened up to connect with Jeff again. Jeff came through and explained that he was not speaking in the personality of eight-year-old Jeff any longer, but was interested in working with me as a guide and teacher if I wanted to. I did. I did not have a focus or direction in the work at first, and simply asked questions that came to me, either personal or philosophical.

At this time I also began working with Edward Bickford, a body/energy worker who had heard of my experiences at The Monroe Institute. He would provide the name of a client and I would provide, though channeled-writing, emotional or psychic case histories about the clients, which he used as background information in working with them. Channeling case histories of people I did not know became part of my life. Occasionally friends would ask for readings, and I obliged. Often it would occur to me that I could let the information I receive flow through and simply be spoken aloud, rather than written. Yet, each time I tried to follow this impetus it felt somewhat awkward for me. It seemed even more uncomfortable for the person I had sitting with me as the witness. Thus, continuing with channeling-through-writing seemed the most comfortable and easily available route. After the Gateway, I knew very strongly there had to be a way for me to bring the focus of metaphysics into the mainstream of my life.

Often when I was working on the foil-wrapping of a stained glass project, a repetitious part of the craft, I would sort of drift in a meditative way. It came to me very strongly that I should open a metaphysical bookstore. How or where wasn't clear, but the idea was. When I shared this inspiration with Perry he, too, felt it was a good project. Yet, here we were in rural Virginia, with a two and a half year old son and a house we were still renovating! There already a metaphysical bookstore in nearby Charlottesville and the area couldn't support another. Yet, following that inner sense, I went ahead. I wrote letters, filled out forms, eventually began ordering books, filling our den with book stock for a shop that did not yet exist in any way. Synchronicity, the idea that there is meaning in coincidence, kept occurring. Support through money, people, ideas, etc., kept coming into our lives. We could feel the flow leading, and we were willing to flow with it.

In June of 1983, we opened *Synchronicity Bookshop* in Washington, D.C. My sister, Jacqui Menkes, committed her support to us to the extent that she drove to Washington from Philadelphia to work at the bookshop three days a week! In time, we were all living in Washington. The bookshop was a wonderful element in our lives. All who became part of this venture grew, expanded, and blossomed. We found a niche in the Washington, D.C. spiritual community. We became known for our friendly, intimate atmosphere, for quartz crystals, for stocking the unusual. It was a special place and time.

I continued my keyboard channeling on an irregular basis, mostly whenever I was asked for a reading. Interestingly, whenever a long gap of time had passed, someone would ask me to do a reading. The ability to channel was present and my universe would step in and remind me of it again and again. By the summer of 1984, thoughts of working with voice channeling came to me more often and consistently. One afternoon I decided to relax and work with a Monroe Institute tape designed to create an open state, a free flow. It was a quiet afternoon. I was home alone in cool air-conditioned comfort (a special thing in sultry Washington!). I lay down on my bed, adjusted my headphones, and promptly drifted into a relaxed state. After a time I heard someone speaking in my room. Eventually I realized it was myself speaking aloud. I realized I was channeling! I was telling myself out loud to call my sister Jacqui, who lived down the hall. I got up, still in a semi-trance state, telephoned her and waited by the door.

I later learned that when Jacqui arrived I looked very strange indeed, standing there in what was obviously an altered state. She, of course, knew of my other experiences and didn't find it too odd to suddenly be involved in a channeling experience. Jacqui had, in fact, introduced me to the world of metaphysics through her first astrology studies when we were teenagers. It was appropriate for her to be there at what was to be the beginning of a major element in my life.

I returned to the trance state and Jacqui began to question the energy beings I was channeling. They said they were not of the Earth, yet not from another planet. They described themselves as being of another 'realm' and were as acting as a link. The said there was a group of energies wishing to work with me. Was I now ready to consider working as a channel? Eventually we understood they were the first step to Orion. The words came slowly and quietly and I felt aligned and comfortable with the experience. I had a knowing of the appropriateness of it all. I also realized my channeling ability was going to continue to come forth until I allowed myself to explore it.

Synchronicity once again stepped in, leading to highly appropriate connections at just the right times. Soon after this channeling experience, I talked with a friend, wondering just how I could open up to the channeling experience. He introduced me to a man who had worked with a channel for almost ten years. We met for lunch, talked, connected and finally made arrangements to get together to try an exploratory session of channeling. It was during this session that Orion came present. Slowly, yet clearly, they answered our questions. The strongest feeling of safety and protection came over me. I felt a sense of recognition and connection. I did not need to know consciously every element of what the future of working with Orion would hold. In a deep fulfilling place I knew I was embracing this relationship.

Orion described how what I call the 'greater I', had chosen before my birth the ability to participate in channeling work. They told how my physical body was attuned, on the molecular and cellular level to work with, receive, and transmit their types of energy. They assured me that the final choice of entering into this work would always come through my conscious agreement and interaction. This choice and commitment could be redirected, rearranged or renegotiated according to my needs and desires whenever I chose.

At this time Michael Gritz was working part-time in the Synchronicity Bookshop. He was a mutual friend of one of my closest friends. Francine had talked of Michael for a long time before we finally met in person, and when he and I did meet, we immediately and powerfully clicked. Michael became one of my closest friends. As we talked about my channeling experiences, it came to me to ask Michael if he would be comfortable working with me to explore channeling. He was not only comfortable, but eager. His own interest in channeling was long-standing. Our connecting as channel and what we came to call, monitor or grounder, was a key element in facilitating the Orion work.

Michael and I began working with Orion and at once, he felt his own connection with the beings we were conversing with. Michael was comfortable with and in-synch with them. We also recognized the depth of the friendship connection between the two of us. This strong sense of interconnections created a comfort level between all of us, which supported the channeling process. In the beginning, I would go into the trance state in a prone position, reflecting techniques I learned at The Monroe Institute. Working with Michael, I soon moved to a sitting position, eventually being able to walk around in the trance state with Orion present. At first I would channel three different voices, individual elements of the group. We then asked for a single voice, a spokesperson, and this served well.

After a time, Orion clarified for us exactly how Michael was adding a particular element to our work. We already knew Michael's presence created a more comfortable feeling for me. We felt it was necessary to have someone present to ask questions, to participate in the discussion with Orion. I could hold questions in my mind and channel the responses into a tape recorder by myself, but *Orion* seemed most interested in working in an interactive relationship with questions and answers and discussion.

Orion explained that Michael also was doing unconscious energy work with my physical body. He would sense tiredness in my body and send thoughts and energy of support. When we began giving readings for people, Michael would act as the link between the person and Orion, literally introducing the person to Orion. We worked in this way, unchanged, for more than three years. Our lives

168

became more complex, and eventually I began to see individual clients without Michael as monitor. We still prefer to work as a team for lectures, classes, and seminars. Michael and I continued our close friendship and working relationship. Michael became part of our family: close friend to my husband, Perry; Godfather to our son, Alexander. Michael and Orion established a true and unique friendship of their own with both of us, all of us. My way of relating personally with Orion is in a more merged state. Michael's experience was more present – talking with them, sharing with them, joking with them.

It was through Michael that we received the name, Orion. We had been working with them for a time, when we asked for their name. They told Michael he would receive a name in meditation. Michael allowed this receptivity, but a name did not come. During a subsequent session, Orion asked Michael what name he had received. He began to say he had not received a name, when 'Orion' popped into his head. 'Is it Orion?' he asked. They acknowledged that Orion was a fine name indeed. They clarified that Orion was a symbolic name. They themselves did not use 'namings' to identify themselves. They further clarified that the name did not relate specifically to the constellation Orion and that they were not from that region or area in the universe.

Yet, the earthly symbols of Orion were present. We later learned that the constellation Orion was in the sky at that time. A short time later we received a book which had a depiction of the myth of Orion who was a giant punished by the gods and aided by a mortal, who rode upon his shoulders. We found the theme of interaction, cooperation, and joint effort coming to us in the various symbols of Orion again and again. These were the very themes Orion emphasized in their material. Orion asked us to form a class of people interested in exploring another perspective of awareness. Michael and I asked among our close circle of friends, and seven of us met for the first class, which we came to call the Core Class. The group of seven included Michael and me, Perry, and four other close friends. In that first class we met approximately every other week for a year. Another year later, with a few changes, the Core Class came together again for another series of classes with Orion. It was from this first group that The Orion material began to grow.

Early on, Orion guided me to create my own 'contract of service' with them. Tuning in and using a kind of free-association, I listed all the qualities that I wanted and did not want as part of my relationship with them. I did not want my physical form to be affected by the work. I did not want negative reactions to channeling and my work with Orion to impact myself and my family. I wanted to always work with others through alignment. I examined the fears and concerns that arose in my thoughts and dreams and addressed them with Orion. In discovering and noting my own requirements, I aligned with Orion's interest in accountability and exchange between realms.

Eventually, through word of mouth, people heard about the Orion work. I was hesitant at first to have consultations with people I didn't know. In the beginning most of our clients were friends of people I knew. Those first sessions were done on a barter basis.

Friends would take us to lunch in exchange for a session. Another friend would exchange a massage. In time, someone wanted a session who was not a friend of a friend. Until then, the Orion work had mostly been a private and personal aspect of my life.

Jim Greene, of 'The Quartet' at The Gateway, counseled me. He asked me if I was willing to share the Orion work. Was I willing to become a public person, known as a channel? Jim encouraged me to share the work and make it available. Jim helped me see that there was an element of service in a willingness to share the experience of Orion in an accessible and public fashion.

There is vulnerability in being a public person, especially in such an unusual and often disparaged arena. The first months I began to see clients, I had many dreams of being hurt or dying because of my spiritual beliefs. In some I was killed for precognition, in others stoned for being a witch, exiled as a shaman; the weaver who didn't believe in the church of the times. In the work with my massage therapist, this same theme would come up in session after session. My mind would fill with these images of pain and destruction. At times, my massage therapist would also receive the same images. We felt these images were aspects of other life expressions – all my fears and memories coming present now through my decision to work publicly as a channel, allowing myself to be vulnerable once again.

This process of releasing fears came present again, but less intensely, during the production of this book. A book represents another level of vulnerability and personal exposure. Orion assured me from the

171

beginning of our relationship that those kinds of experiences would not be repeated. They guided me to always use my inner sensing when sharing with people what I do. Orion encouraged me to trust my feelings of whom to share with and how much to share, saying I would sense those who were receptive. An aura of support from them was always there, no matter how subtle or unrecognized by me.

Following this inner sense led me to have conversations about Orion, channeling, other realities, etc., with many individuals I would not have consciously thought of as receptive. These included such people as bank tellers, office supply salesmen, tax accountants, and society matrons. Usually I would begin by saying I taught classes in metaphysics. At the next level, I would share that I gave a type of psychic reading. Actually, being a psychic these days is interesting to people, not disconcerting. Yet, working as a channel is often experienced as too much to comprehend. But, oh so many times, I would begin talking about my metaphysical classes and the least likely individual would draw more in-depth information from me.

Such encounters demonstrated to me again and again a main facet of the Orion work, which is that people expressing their spiritual impulse in life need share no specific vocabulary, no outward appearances, no dietary focus, specific religion or belief system. On the whole, my experience with people concerning the Orion work has been supportive and positive. I learned ways to balance the energy of interacting with many people. I learned as well to balance the energy of Elisabeth, the private person; wife and mother, artist, opera lover, film buff, etc. and Elisabeth, the trance-channel and public person. I am not two separate beings, but sometimes it is beneficial and balanced for these aspects of my life to have separate moments and times of focus.

Occasionally I wondered at the seeming incongruity that spiritual exploration became a dominant focus of my life, at a time which seemed to be more for settling in, making a home, raising a child. In retrospect, and with insight from Orion, I came to see that perhaps it was those very elements in my life - my marriage, my child, renovating the house, etc. - that were acting as a grounding factor. This grounding served as a foundation supporting the wide circles of thought and experience I was exploring. Even as I found myself again and again stepping out of daily reality, following an inner sense over logic, I could always use my everyday reality as a way of staying balanced. The personal world of my family and close friends serve as a key to the integration of the expanded and the mundane. I also use my family life as a guide for priorities, as a balancing element in decisions about how I work.

The Orion work has led its own direction and growth. After a time of doing client sessions, people began to ask for a way to learn more about Orion's perspective in general, and the lecture series began with small groups meeting in my home. Classes and seminars followed, and now, this book.

Working with Orion is for me, in the most personal way, a gift, a joy and a treasure in my life. It is always a gift when you find a particular thrust in life which calls you and you discover you can meet the call. Sharing the gift with others has had its stresses and pressures, but the impetus to share has been stronger. Orion in their manner of being, with their caring and sensitive energy, as well as their light-hearted humor, have been a special joy to know, but more so, their perspective and the way it has expanded my own views, is an experience of such intensity and power, that the need to share it is compelling.

Knowing Orion has led me to experience, again and again, connection. Being part of a whole is present with me always. I can touch into Unity whenever I need to, whenever I ask and reach out. I experience in my daily life an acute awareness of the elements which connect us all to each other, to the nature kingdoms, to Spirit. Orion touches me, has guided me and given me tools to touch more than myself. Perhaps, you too, shall share some of my experience of Orion.

Elisabeth Y. Fitzhugh

Washington, D.C. 1987

CONTINUING WITH ORION

20 YEARS WITH ORION

When I opened to working with Orion I had no precognition, no inkling, that I had entered into a relationship, a work, an expression, that would easily and naturally flow into the next quarter century of my life and perhaps, for the entire duration of my life. I had no sense that the interaction would be for a short or proscribed sense of time either. Rather, I definitely did have the sense that I had opened to a true exploration, a journey where I could sense the moment, at times sense the next direction, and at other times, be at ease with following the flow and discovering where I would be next.

Each movement of the Orion work has evolved with a natural feel and pace. Synchronicity has been the byword. Personal sessions led to lectures, lectures led to classes, transcribing the material led to the book. Technology brought personal sessions by telephone, with long-term clients of many years, who I have yet to meet in person. Telephone classes bring together individuals all over the country in intimate shared meetings. The internet offers a continuing presence for people to discover and explore the Orion work all over the world at any time of the day and is a vibrant expression of the reality of the true web of interconnection that we

175

are all part of and expressions of. The Internet reflects to us the essence of Unity consciousness everyday.

The outer forms of the Orion work have had variation. At times of my life, I have taken summers off of all public work. At other times, I might do personal sessions, but not classes or workshops or lectures. Yet, the Orion connection is a constant in my life. The intimate one-on-one personal sessions seem to be the true foundation of the Orion work. However hectic or focused my life might become in other ways, eventually there will be a call for a personal session that returns me to the sharing of the *Orion* experience.

Naturally, my personal life has had many shifts in the last decades. My husband Perry and I went our separate ways after many years of marriage and are still supportive friends. New partnership and support came to me with my husband, Dennis Galumbeck. Life took me back to Central Virginia after many years in Washington, DC. I now live in the small city of Waynesboro, Virginia, a place I find most nurturing and supportive, in the beautiful Shenandoah Valley at the edge of the Blue Ridge Mountains. Yet, Washington, DC has remained the home of the public work with Orion, in the form of lectures and workshops.

A few years ago I dealt with what eventually was diagnosed as two non-invasive breast cancer tumors. Treatment involved two lumpectomies and radiation. As you might imagine, this experience took me to a new depth in living spiritual awareness. Though Orion was present as an underlying support, I had to journey through the experience myself. Like many people who find they must deal with illness, I had to face the possibility of death. This was most present with me during the two weeks I waited for the pathology report on my biopsy. Invasive breast cancer is a higher risk and typically requires more treatment such as chemotherapy, than a non-invasive tumor; the pathology report would tell me what I was about to face.

It was there that I came to a still knowing place, that no matter what I would have to face, I had available to me the capacity to be with it, to live with it and through it, no matter how difficult the journey or where it would take me. I have spoken with other people who have faced such a crossroad and almost everyone has shared their own version of recognizing that in this life of interconnection, this sense of strength, of the capacity for being with life is available.

Orion is present with me in an incredibly supportive way, but typically they are non-directive. In most situations, after I have found my own way, they share further insight on the situation. This was so during this pathology waiting period, but there was a previous moment where they stepped out of their retrospective insight role and came more present. New recommendations had come out that women could have mammograms every two years instead of every year. I was considering this option, when one night before bed, Orion distinctly said, 'Have the mammogram as usual.'

I didn't feel any particular trepidation about their recommendation, but did strongly feel I should follow the advice. This was the very mammogram where the cancer was detected. As it turned out, the sites of my tumors were so small they were not actually visible on the mammogram itself. There was just enough to indicate that there could be a tumor or something benign like a cyst or calcification, so a biopsy was in order. In the end, I feel most blessed that these tumors were revealed at the earliest possible stage, rather than a year later if I had followed my first plan.

Working with Orion has created a solid foundation of perspective. I do comprehend the world enhanced by their sensibility, which I am immersed in. I find as well, as they said at the beginning, that we are always in exchange and I can see how the interests and experiences that have come into my life can be used as examples or demonstrations by Orion. I have always felt that part of my work with them is to be the living demonstration of applying the principles and insights they have shared.

Like others, I have at times had one step forward and one step back. Like others, I can sometimes see things in retrospect that I was unable to bring forward in the moment. But I have thrived and flourished on the vitality of living spiritual awareness as a growing, evolving energy. I feel we are always growing and expanding and in that, there is no need to want to feel done or complete or perfect in any idealistic way. Orion shares that such evolution of consciousness is a continuum, now and beyond the time of our physical now. Beginning once again is the natural flow of life.

Integration is a primary principle Orion shares. They often refer to integration as how we knit together our understandings and experiences to see something in another way. I also experience integration in the many ways my life finds expression, along with the work with Orion. Relationship and friendship are key focuses of time and energy. My dear friend Helen and I meet weekly in my art studio for a concentrated day of work. My husband and I enjoy lively restaurants, movies and travel. And throughout everything, are the hours of conversation with each other, Helen and other friends, inquiring into and exploring together our ideas and understandings of life and its continuing shifts and changes.

In the end, I have been given a great gift in this relationship with this expansive consciousness we call Orion. I experience them as their own energy, distinct from mine, always honoring, of course, that we are all interconnected. Their friendship has been consistent in every way. Patient, caring, respectful and honoring as well. It has been another delight that I have been able to share their presence and work. It is beautiful that there are so many others who have their own personal relationship with and experience of Orion.

In a recent lecture, Orion referred to the group as a 'gathering of a clan.' They said it was an open, inviting clan; a gathering where we could be with and recognize each other and the connection that is inherent in being. Perhaps it is through what we can sense and feel in our personal gatherings of clan that we can add to the evolution of the consistent recognition of the true connection of clan – that we are all one; that Unity consciousness is the true nature of reality. I hope sharing my experience may speak to you in some small way and that together, in living our lives with the idea of Unity, we can support the recognition of the interconnection of all things.

Elisabeth Y. Fitzhugh
Waynesboro, Virginia   2007

GLOSSARY

ACCOUNTABILITY

A deep spiritual willingness to stand by, and be answerable for, one's ideas, decisions, and actions in daily life as well as in the spiritual life. *See Axioms of Awareness.*

AFFIRM (TO AFFIRM)

To make or acknowledge a deep statement of desire, belief, awareness.

AFFIRMATION

A phrase or statement used as a tool to acknowledge and bring into focus a desire, belief, or intent of awareness.

ALL THERE IS

The known and unknown Universe in its totality; physical and spiritual life in every aspect. *See Unity.*

ALIGNMENT

When the energies surrounding a situation, experience, understanding, etc. come into agreement and connection. *See Axioms of Awareness.*

ALLOWING (& PERMITTING)

An approach or technique in which one does not coerce or direct a decision or outcome with the conscious mind, but allows time for the situation to come into alignment through its own patterns. *See Axioms of Awareness.*

ATTUNEMENT

A sense of intense alignment, where all aspects of a being -- Inner Awareness, Conscious Awareness and the outer world -- come into interconnection and agreement. *See Working With Awareness.*

AWARENESS

A state of knowing that encompasses conscious knowledge and knowing from sources beyond the physical senses.

AXIOMS

Statements of principles of awareness. In the Orion perspective, the axioms are seen as consistent principles related to understanding the nature of aware being. *See Axioms of Awareness.*

BALANCING

The idea that balance is not a static state to be achieved, but a fluid, moving state to be experienced as action. *See Aware Living.*

BELIEF STRUCTURE

The system of understanding you draw to yourself and express from all your knowledge, conscious and beyond, interwoven with the customs and understandings of your time and place. *See Aware Living.*

BLEED-THROUGH (SEE SEALING)

In the concept of other lives/past lives, a time or situation when energy, information, feelings, etc. from another life influence the current life without conscious understanding that such an influence is occurring. Sealing is a technique to balance bleed-through. *See Esoterica.*

CHANNELING

A process of strong receptivity whereby one allows connection with information, awareness, or energies outside of the physical, conscious self and allows that energy, etc., to flow through the physical body and be expressed. *See Introduction: On Channeling.*

CO-CREATION

Rooted in the idea that we are interconnected with All There Is, we create aspects of reality but we do not create the totality of reality through conscious will alone. Co-creation honors that there are forces of creation at work that one does not consciously or unconsciously comprehend. *See Spiritual Awareness.*

CONNECTEDNESS

A linking - consciously, spiritually, physically – of people, situations, nature, realities etc. Recognition of being connected to All There Is. *See Unity.*

CONSCIOUS AWARENESS (i.e., EGO AWARENESS)

That part of a being that represents the conscious, logical, personality self, including the psychological/emotional aspects as well as what is referred to in psychological terms, as 'the unconscious.' The part of the being which learns through the physical senses, concrete information, etc. *See Unity.*

CORE AWARENESS

That part of a being connected to the Core Essence, to the Unity, through which one can access information and awareness from beyond the Conscious self. *See Unity.*

CORE ESSENCE

Rooted in the concept of Unity, the Core Essence is that aspect of All There Is each of us inherently possesses and through which we link and experience 'All There Is.' *See Unity.*

DISCERNMENT

A balanced approach to perceiving and understanding preferences, choices and options, without moving into judgment. *See Axioms of Awareness.*

DRAMA

Limiting oneself to creating dramatic, intense, often unsettling and painful situations, as a method of bringing about change and growth. *See Working with Awareness.*

EARTH MATRIX

The core of your being committed to living in this time and place - Earth and all it encompasses – its physical structure, the nature elements, our cultures and history. *See Esoterica.*

EMPIRICAL HISTORY OF AWARENESS

Using your own life and its experiences to consistently demonstrate and affirm to yourself the principles of awareness.

ENERGIES

Used as a plural for the idea of energy – pulsations of interconnection; also used to describe beings who are not in physical form.

ENERGIZE/ENERGIZATION

To consciously bring your intent and focus to setting directions and working with energy for specific goals, focuses, ideas, etc. Energization is akin to an affirmation.

ENERGY

A term to describe the form in which the pulsations of interconnection, of being, of All There Is, occurs.

EXPANDED AWARENESS

The part of the being that experiences connection to All There Is and through which one gathers information, understanding etc., from all aspects of being. Can also be understood as the Soul, Spirit Self, etc. *See Unity.*

FLOW (THE/TO)

Representing the movement of the energy patterns within all aspects of life. 'To flow' is expressing the principle in conscious action.

GIFT (TO GIFT)

An offering to the self or to another, usually with a deep spiritual understanding and knowing, often not consciously recognized. 'To gift' is expressing the principle in conscious action. One can gift attitudes, acceptance, understanding, etc.

GUIDES

The idea that there are energies that serve as a support or guide to a person. These guides can be energies or beings from outside the self; they can be aspects of the present self, the past self and more. *See Esoterica.*

HOLISTIC/WHOLISTIC

A view of living that acknowledges the interconnections of all things; the wholeness of life, one aspect having an effect on another.

HONORING/TO HONOR

Self-respect with a spiritual base whereby one acknowledges and accepts elements of perfection, attainment of wisdom, etc., within the self. To honor takes the principle into conscious action. *See Spiritual Awareness.*

ICONS/IMAGES

Symbols and images that you create, allow and discover to use as tools of focus for exploration, understanding, or creation. *See Working With Awareness.*

INNER AWARENESS

A sensing aspect of the being similar to Core Awareness; that part of a being connected to Unity through which you can access information and awareness from beyond the Conscious self. *See Unity.*

INTEGRATION

Weaving together spiritual views and understandings with everyday choices, actions, and beliefs. *See Axioms of Awareness.*

INTERCONNECTEDNESS

Reflecting the Unity; all the energies of life are connected with and within each other. *See Unity.*

LIFE EXPRESSION

The expression of the Core Essence, i.e., Soul, as a lifetime, as in 'past lives or future lives.' *See Esoterica.*

LIGHT (THE)

A symbolic word/icon to describe the Core Essence of the Universe, of All There Is, as in Spirit.

LINK (TO LINK)

The Link represents the connectedness of all things; 'to link' is the conscious initiating and allowing of connection.

LONG HAUL

Applying spiritual awareness to the whole of ones life. *See Axioms of Awareness.*

MODULATION

A process where one communicates beliefs and approaches in a non-confrontational manner as a conscious tool of communication. *See Aware Living.*

MUNDANE

Referring to the daily events and rhythms of living. *See Working with Awareness.*

MULTIVERSE

The concept that the Universe is not a singular aspect, as in uni or one, but is a moving web of many aspects of being and existence, as in multi or multiple. *See Foreword 2nd Edition.*

OPTION

The variety of choices, opportunities, directions available; not limited to one choice or another. *See Axioms of Awareness.*

OTHER LIVES/PAST LIVES

Stemming from the concept that the Core Essence or Soul of a being creates expressions of that Core Essence through lifetimes of experience. Other Lives/Past Lives refers to the further idea that in the continuum of life one may experience more than the present self; thus having lives in the past, future or out of the concept of time. *See Esoterica.*

PARADOX

Elements of life that seem contradictory or opposite or nullifying, but exist at the same time.

PARAMETERS

The variables one uses to base options and choices upon, as in your belief system or understanding. *See Axioms of Awareness.*

PSYCHOLOGICAL MATRIX

Seen as part of the Conscious Awareness, the part of one's psyche that reflects the emotions and experiences of this lifetime, including the psychologically-termed, 'unconscious.' *See Unity.*

RESONATE

To feel, experience and recognize a connection with information, people, situations, etc.; to recognize alignment. *See Axioms of Awareness.*

RESPOND-ABILITY

An extrapolated definition of responsibility, meaning one has the ability to respond to a situation, commitment, etc. *See Axioms of Awareness.*

RETROSPECT

Looking into the past from the vantage point of the present, to gain more complete understanding of what transpired, what interconnections were experienced, etc. *See Tools of Awareness.*

SENSING/SENSING AWARENESS

A gathering of knowledge, information and awareness that involves more than using the physical senses and logical deduction; information flows through the sensing ability of the Triad of Awareness, based on the concept of Unity. *See Unity.*

SHADINGS

Referring to the subtleties of a situation, i.e., the tones and shades as in the differences in a color. *See Working with Awareness.*

SINGULAR

As in only one possible approach or way of being.

SOURCE

As in the Source of all being, Source Energy, i.e., Spirit, All There Is, God.

SPIRITUAL EXPRESSION

How one expresses, lives, shares the Core Essence, the connection to Unity in ones life. *See Spiritual Awareness.*

SPIRITUAL PRACTICES

The focuses you choose or discover to express your spiritual beliefs, such as meditation, prayer, organized religious systems, food preferences, etc. *See Spiritual Awareness.*

SPIRITUAL PIONEERS

Individuals living their daily lives integrated with spiritual principles; often choosing to share their ideas and approaches with others. *See Spiritual Awareness.*

STRUCTURE

A system outside the self, as in a foundation or armature, used to support development and growth. Systems are as varied as commitment, such as marriage; focus, as in a job or career; beliefs as in religious practice, etc. *See Relating Through Awareness.*

SYNCHRONICITY

The concept that there can be meaning in coincidence; that coincidence reflects interconnectedness, linking through the Web. Term was first used by Carl Jung.

TOOL/TOOLS

Practical approaches and techniques as well as conceptual ideas that are used to achieve or further understanding and to create or allow change. *See Tools of Awareness.*

TRIAD OF AWARENESS

The Orion conceptualization of the interconnected elements of Consciousness within a being, i.e., the Conscious Awareness, the Inner Awareness, the Expanded Awareness. *See Unity.*

UNITY

The core of all being; the connectedness of all things; a connection shared and able to be experienced by all life.   *See Unity.*

WEB (THE)

As in the image of a spider's web, the energy web through which the connectedness of all things, linking occurs.   *See Unity.*

Let Language be a tool of expansion.
Allow words the freedom to impart
deep and varied meanings.
Do not use words to bind, but to
support freedom of thought and being.

Heartfelt Acknowledgement to those who were with us at the beginning of the Orion Material journey: Michael Gritz, Jacqui Menkes, Francine Cohen, Donna Anahata, David Hicks, Mimi Fitzhugh, Perry Fitzhugh, to those who helped make the 2nd edition possible: Ellyn Dye, Jane Batt, Bernadette Aukward, Ravile and Arnold Talcott and everyone who shared the questions and experiences that are the heart of the Orion Material.

Special Thoughts to those who were part of the Orion journey and are no longer with us: friend and mentor Jim Greene and the magical Martha Leigh, of the Gateway Quartet, Dave Wallis, who introduced me to the Monroe Institute; Oscar Garcia-Vera, Patricia Serino, Christian Crislip and my father, Anthony V. Yannucci, whose presence in his final days so strongly imbued the final manuscript of the 1987 first edition *Orion Material – Perspectives of Awareness*.

And Special Thanks to those who helped bring this 20th Anniversary edition together: as always, my ever-supportive husband, Dennis Galumbeck, my dear friend and cohort Helen Seline and the special cadre of editors, proof-readers, designers, ideas and support people: April McGuigan, Deb Booth, Benn Kobb, Forest Jones, Laura English Jones, Leslie France, Justin X. Frank, Steve T.H. Sawmelle and Teresa Rogovsky.

Elisabeth Fitzhugh has been sharing the Orion experience for over twenty years. Long attracted to understanding the nature of things, Elisabeth came to her exploration of spiritual awareness through studies in psychology, anthropology and art. *Synchronicity Press* was founded in 1987 to make the Orion material available and other titles supporting spiritual awareness and exploration.

If you are drawn to know more about the ongoing work with the Orion

consciousness including our free quarterly e-newsletter,

personal sessions and workshops,

please visit us at

www.orionwisdom.us

Also by the author –

Dancers Between Realms –
Empath Energy, *Beyond Empathy*

Box 1154
Waynesboro, Virginia 22980 USA
www.synchronicitypress.com

Synchronicity –
the sense of significance beyond chance

We are all together.
We are all linked.
We are all inherently part of
All There Is.
Therein lies our strength,
wisdom, and compassion.
Unity is.